RAND NATIONAL DEFENSE RESEARCH INSTITUTE

Meeting the Language and Culture Training Needs of U.S. Department of Defense Personnel

An Evaluation of the Language Training Center Program

Jennifer J. Li, Richard S. Girven, Norah Griffin

Prepared for the Office of the Secretary of Defense

Approved for public release; distribution unlimited

For more information on this publication, visit www.rand.org/t/RR2555

Library of Congress Cataloging-in-Publication Data is available for this publication.
ISBN: 978-1-9774-0242-4

Published by the RAND Corporation, Santa Monica, Calif.

Cover photo: Concordia Language Training Center.

Preface

In 2011, Section 529 of the National Defense Authorization Act for Fiscal Year 2010 established the Language Training Center (LTC) Program to leverage the expertise and infrastructure of institutions of higher education to train U.S. Department of Defense (DoD) personnel in language, culture, and regional area studies. In October 2013, DoD submitted a report to the congressional defense committees on the status of the LTC Program, as mandated by Section 529(e) of the legislation. The report covered progress and activities by the LTCs at accredited institutions of higher education from the start of the program in fall 2011 through September 2013. At that time, the Department recommended continuation of the program for three additional years, at which time a reevaluation of the program's efficacy and viability as a permanent program could be undertaken.

The Defense Language and National Security Education Office (DLNSEO) asked the RAND Corporation to conduct the reevaluation of the LTC Program, which included centers at nine universities in the fiscal year 2017 grant cycle. This report provides the findings of the evaluation study and recommendations to enhance the program moving forward.

This report should be of interest to DoD, DLNSEO, and LTC Program directors and staff and sponsor organizations involved in language, regional education, and culture programs. This research was sponsored by DLNSEO and conducted within the Forces and Resources Policy Center of the RAND National Defense Research Institute, a federally funded research and development center sponsored by the Office of the Secretary of Defense, the Joint Staff, the Unified Combatant Commands, the Navy, the Marine Corps, the defense agencies, and the defense Intelligence Community.

For more information on the RAND Forces and Resources Policy Center, see www.rand.org/nsrd/ndri/centers/frp or contact the director (contact information is provided on the webpage).

Contents

Figure and Tables

Figure

Tables

Summary

History and Research Design

The Language Training Center (LTC) Program was established in 2011 under Section 529 of the National Defense Authorization Act for Fiscal Year 2010. The program's purpose is to leverage the expertise and infrastructure of institutions of higher education to train U.S. Department of Defense (DoD) personnel in language, culture, and regional area studies. In October 2013, DoD submitted a report to the congressional defense committees on the status of the LTC Program, as mandated by Section 529(e) of the legislation. The report covered progress and activities by the LTCs at accredited institutions of higher education from the start of the program in the fall of 2011 through September 2013. At that time, the Department recommended continuation of the program for three additional years, at which time a reevaluation of the program's efficacy and viability as a permanent program could be undertaken.

In 2016, the Defense Language and National Security Education Office (DLNSEO) asked the RAND Corporation to conduct the reevaluation of the LTC Program, which included centers at nine universities in the fiscal year (FY) 2017 grant cycle. It is important to note that DLNSEO asked RAND to examine the *LTC Program overall*, rather than to conduct individual evaluations of each of the nine LTCs within the program. Given the priorities of DLNSEO and the available data, we addressed the following questions:

1. Is the LTC Program fulfilling the mandate of the legislation?
2. How are LTCs leveraging the existing infrastructure for language instruction at institutions of higher education?
3. What practices are in place, and where are there opportunities for improvement?
4. How can the LTC Program improve its metrics and assessments?
5. What factors affect how the LTCs use the funds provided?

To answer these questions, we reviewed the legislation that created the LTC Program, the 2013 DoD report to Congress, grant-cycle requests for proposals from LTCs, and other documents related to the establishment and administration of the LTCs. Researchers conducted site visits to all nine LTCs to understand the processes and training provided by the LTCs. Through site visits and phone meetings, we conducted 136 interviews with key LTC stakeholders, then we analyzed the available information about the overarching program and individual programs to answer the above questions where possible and identify where LTC practices are working well and where there are opportunities for improvement. Based on this descriptive, qualitative study, we offer recommendations for DLNSEO, the LTCs, and the Institute of International Education (IIE) to consider as they continue to implement and grow the LTC Program.

Key Findings

The LTC Program is fulfilling its mandate. We found that, overall, the LTC Program is meeting the vast majority of the requirements of its authorizing legislation. The program is building skills in language and area studies from beginning through advanced levels; it provides language training in critical and strategic languages for operational readiness; and it uses alternative language training delivery systems to provide training to a wide variety of DoD partners. In the 2017 grant year, the LTC Program provided more than 200 courses to more than 1,450 students, covering 15 languages as well as culture and regional studies.[1]

The infrastructure at institutions of higher education provides LTCs benefits, but with trade-offs. We found that being situated in institutions of higher education provides LTCs a number of benefits, including, but not limited to, access to scholars and experts in languages, pedagogy, and area studies; access to facilities and resources; and instant credibility with DoD partners looking for quality instruction. Association with institutions of higher education, however, does come with trade-offs—such as calendar conflicts and the bureaucratic processes of, for example, finance and human resources departments, which may be slow.

As expected, LTC practices vary, with room for improvement to encourage a more cohesive and collaborative professional community. Given that the program is meant to allow for flexibility and innovation, we were not surprised to find a wide variety in courses, styles of training, and approaches to key aspects of implementation, such as ensuring teaching quality, measuring performance, and use of grant funds. We found that LTCs vary widely in how they train and evaluate their instructors, which suggests that a variety of standards and expectations are being applied. We heard that some teachers felt the need to develop their own materials, and some expressed reluctance to share information with other teachers or other LTCs.

LTCs varied in how they measured outcomes. We found that DLNSEO, IIE, and the LTCs all recognize the importance of measuring outcomes, but they do it in different ways. Variation is to be expected (and even desired) due to the nature of the

1 IIE, *Language Training Center Overview*, New York, 2017.

LTC Program, but there are some areas in which consistency could be encouraged, where appropriate, to enable DLNSEO and DoD stakeholders to better understand the results being attained by the LTCs and compare them across centers.

Variations in LTC capacity utilization suggest that DoD partners are not taking full advantage of the program. We found that most LTCs were able to utilize all or nearly all of the funds granted, and a small number of LTCs spent below award levels. We observed that the LTCs with stronger relationships and more frequent communication with their DoD partner tended to have higher proportions of course seats filled and therefore higher capacity utilization.

This suggests that some DoD partners were not taking full advantage of the training available to them, despite positive perceptions of the quality of the training. The overall level of capacity utilization across the LTC Program was approximately 80 percent.

Recommendations

Foster a Greater Ongoing Program-Wide Focus on Meaningful Outcomes, Not Just Provision of Training

With the LTC Program now well established in its eighth year of operation, there is an opportunity to strengthen the program and ensure its positive impact by increasing the focus on the outcomes of LTC training rather than merely on the provision of training. The program has demonstrated its ability to provide hundreds of courses per year to meet the needs of 24 DoD partners and more than 1,450 students in a single grant year. A next step in the program's development could be for it to place further emphasis on the importance of measuring training outcomes and to use the information to engage in deliberate and ongoing cycles of continuous improvement. As of the grant year that ended in 2017, some LTCs were assessing their own performance through assessments of student outcomes, and some were doing so primarily by whether they had provided the training requested of them. Further, the LTC Program overall reports its outcomes in terms of provision (i.e., numbers of courses provided and number of students who received training), which is a reasonable first step.

Moving forward, we recommend that DLNSEO and IIE encourage the LTCs that are not yet measuring training outcomes to articulate objectives that go beyond provision and represent meaningful proficiency, skill, or knowledge outcomes for the DoD partners and students served by each LTC. This process could be done initially through a pilot phase dedicated to identifying appropriate, meaningful, and measurable outcomes for each of the respective centers. Following the pilot phase, identifying and reporting measures of success could become a requirement stated in the request for proposal (RFP) and implemented through the course of normal program activities. Although the most recent RFP requested plans for measurement, the plans have not always been implemented. Moving forward, identifying and measuring meaningful outcomes could serve as foundation for continuous improvement. Given the variety of training across the program, we are not recommending that a single metric be applied across all LTCs. Those that provide unique training will need to have metrics suited to their courses. However, in the cases where multiple LTCs are providing comparable training, the program may wish to establish common metrics. This will allow DLNSEO and the LTCs to better understand the extent to which they are meeting their goals. For example, if a DoD partner requests training to sustain language proficiency at a level 2, the measure of success should be the number and proportion of students who achieved level 2 or higher by the end of the course, not simply the number of students who attended and completed the course.

Over Time, Encourage and Build a Culture of Professional Collaboration Among LTCs

We observed that LTCs currently have little interaction with one another outside of the program's annual meeting. Many LTCs expressed interest in the practices of others but perceived little to no means of learning more about them. Importantly, we noticed an undercurrent of competition, which was confirmed by members of the LTC community. At the same time, we observed that some LTCs have more demand for their training than they can accommodate, while other LTCs are under-enrolled. In addition, we saw teachers at various sites working independently on efforts such as developing course materials—sometimes unaware that others were doing nearly the same thing in other LTCs, and sometimes aware but suspicious of collaborating with one another for fear of losing control of their intellectual property.

We recommend that DLNSEO take steps to encourage and foster collaboration over time. Options include providing more in-person meetings, not only for LTC directors but also for their instructional leaders and teaching staffs. Productive purposes for such meetings could be to provide professional development for instructors teaching similar courses at various sites; training for specific certifications, such as oral proficiency interview (OPI) tester training; or workshops in materials development for teachers of languages in which materials are especially limited. Another option would be to incentivize and recognize staff members from more-established and demonstrably successful LTCs who provide coaching, mentoring, and/or guidance to staff members at newer LTCs. Such steps to enhance collaboration and professional learning program-wide may help reduce the underlying sense of competition and, over time, lead to a professional community more likely to sustain itself if and when the grant program is reduced or ended.

Explore Ways to Help DoD Partners More Fully Utilize the Training Capacity Provided

The LTC Program represents a substantial investment in providing language and culture training to DoD in a way that is flexible and allows for innovation to meet new and changing needs. Program-wide, about 80 percent of the training seats available are being filled. At individual LTCs, the percentage of available seats that are filled ranges from 50 to 100 percent with a median of 80 percent. This reveals that in some LTCs a substantial amount of the capacity for language and culture training is not being utilized. Most commonly, LTCs attributed the lower enrollment numbers simply to DoD partners sending fewer students than originally projected. This could be due to students canceling at the last minute because of job demands, to courses being offered at times that were not convenient to students, or to a DoD partner overestimating the demand for a requested course. It could also be due to a center responding to a request for a course in a language for which the demand is small but critical. For example, a center might offer a requested course to meet the needs of only two or three students, but the course might be able to accommodate up to six students if there were demand. When class sizes are intentionally small, as they are in LTCs, having just one or two students not enroll as planned can make a substantial difference. We note that it is unrealistic to expect 100-percent capacity utilization, given the uncertainties of service members' schedules and their need to be responsive to a range of demands.

We recommend that DLNSEO establish a means to share information about available training with a broader range of DoD entities, so that if the DoD partner that requested the training does not fill the available spaces, other DoD personnel would be able to enroll. Over time, this could lead to greater awareness of LTC training and perhaps to new partnerships and/or increased interest in LTC training.

Looking Ahead

The LTC Program was created to provide language and culture training to DoD personnel from beginning to advanced levels in order to sustain and enhance operational readiness in critical languages, culture, and regional expertise. In the eight years since its inception, the program has grown and demonstrated its ability to provide quality training in a responsive and flexible manner to an increasingly larger population of DoD personnel. The challenges that lie ahead will be to (1) encourage increased consistency across the program in some areas where it makes sense while providing opportunities for uniqueness and creativity at each of the LTCs and (2) increase focus on meaningful measurement of outcomes while continuing to support responsiveness, innovation, and perhaps further growth. The findings of this study should provide LTC policymakers, leaders, staff members, and partners with a base of information to help them successfully plan for and execute the next stage in the development of this important DoD program.

Acknowledgments

We would like to thank the many people in the U.S. Department of Defense, the Defense Language and National Security Education Office, the Institute of International Education, and the language training centers who generously gave of their time and knowledge to help with this research. Without the assistance of the language training center directors and staff, along with many instructors and students, we could not have conducted this study.

We would like to thank Michael Nugent, Sam Eisen, and Shirley Rapues for their direction and support throughout the project. They provided us with invaluable guidance and insights that informed this work in important ways.

We would like to thank our reviewers, Hugh McFarlane and Margaret Tankard. Their helpful and insightful reviews greatly improved the quality of the manuscript.

Finally, we would like to thank John Winkler, director of the RAND Forces and Resources Policy Center, and Lisa Harrington, associate director, for their encouragement and support throughout the project.

Abbreviations

ACTFL	American Council on the Teaching of Foreign Languages
CLPM	command language program manager
DLI	Defense Language Institute
DLNSEO	Defense Language and National Security Education Office
DLPT	Defense Language Proficiency Test
DoD	U.S. Department of Defense
ESL	English as a second language
FAO	foreign area officer
GLOSS	Global Language Online Support System
IHE	institute of higher education
IIE	Institute of International Education
ILR	Interagency Language Roundtable
LTC	Language Training Center
NDAA	National Defense Authorization Act
NSEP	National Security Education Program
OPI	oral proficiency interview
OPIc	oral proficiency interview by computer
RFP	request for proposals
ROTC	Reserve Officer Training Corps
SLA	senior language authority
VTC	video teleconference

CHAPTER ONE

Introduction

The Language Training Center (LTC) program was established in 2011 under Section 529 of the National Defense Authorization Act (NDAA) for Fiscal Year (FY) 2010.[1] The program's purpose is to leverage the expertise and infrastructure of institutes of higher education (IHEs) to train U.S. Department of Defense (DoD) personnel in language, culture, and regional area studies. LTC pilot initiative program grants were initially awarded to five IHEs to demonstrate their ability to meet the quality language and cultural training requirements of specific DoD components.[2] By 2013, the number of educational institutions funded through the LTC initiative had grown to nine.

In October 2013, DoD submitted a comprehensive report to the congressional defense committees on the status of the LTC Program as mandated by Section 529(e) of the enacting legislation.[3] The report provided an assessment of progress and overview of activities by the LTCs at accredited IHEs from the start of the program in the fall of 2011 through September 2013. At that time, DoD recommended continuation of the LTC Program for three additional years, at which time a planned reevaluation of the program's efficacy and viability and its continuation as a permanent program could be undertaken.

In 2016, the Defense Language and National Security Education Office (DLNSEO) asked RAND to undertake the reevaluation and examine the LTC Programs at each of the nine institutions serving as LTCs in the FY 2017 grant cycle and to evaluate the efficacy and long-term value of the overall program.

---

1 Pub. L. No. 111-84, 2009.

2 LTC Program, "History," webpage, undated (b).

3 U.S. Department of Defense, *Language Training Center Program: Report to Congress* (as required by Section 529(e) of the National Defense Authorization Act for Fiscal Year 2010), Washington, D.C., 2013.

Research Objectives and Tasks

DLNSEO asked RAND to assess the LTC Program's effectiveness in meeting its stated objectives and recommend whether the program should be continued as is or modified as appropriate. It is important to note that DLNSEO asked RAND to examine the *LTC Program overall*, rather than to conduct individual evaluations of each of the nine LTCs within the program.[4] DLNSEO asked RAND to address the following questions:

1. Is the LTC Program fulfilling the mandate of the legislation?
2. How are LTCs leveraging the existing infrastructure for language instruction at institutions of higher education?
3. What practices are in place, and where are there opportunities for improvement?
4. How can the LTC Program improve its metrics and assessments?
5. What factors affect how the LTCs use the funds provided?[5]

To answer these questions, we reviewed the legislation that created the LTC Program, the 2013 DoD report to Congress, grant-cycle requests for proposals from LTCs, and other documents related to the establishment and administration of the LTCs. Researchers conducted site visits to all nine LTCs to understand the processes and training provided by the LTCs. Through site visits and phone meetings, we conducted interviews with key LTC stakeholders. Those stakeholders included leaders and staff from DLNSEO and its administrative partner, the Institute of International Education (IIE); ten of the command language program managers (CLPMs) or senior language authorities (SLAs) at DoD partner organizations; leaders, staff, and instructors from all nine of the LTCs; and approximately 70 students from more than two dozen classes across the LTC Program. The classes represent a convenience sample; the research team visited classes at each of the site visits if classes were in session at that location at the time of the site visit. Similarly, we met with instructors based on availability at the time of the site visits. We then analyzed the available information about the overarching program and individual programs to answer the above questions where possible and identify where LTC practices are working well and where there are opportunities for improvement. Given the convenience samples, the findings describe only the available data and do not represent all students and all teachers at all of the LTCs. This

---

4 In this report, we use the term *LTC Program* to refer to the overall program that includes the set of nine LTCs that make up the LTC Program today. When we refer to individual LTCs, we most commonly do not name the specific center or centers. This is consistent with the spirit of the overall study, which was to understand the functioning of the set of LTCs rather than to evaluate them individually.

5 DLNSEO originally asked RAND to assess the cost-effectiveness of the LTC Program, but the available data were not suitable to conduct such an analysis. Instead, we examined another area related to cost, which was the question that appears here.

report provides a summary of the findings from this descriptive, qualitative study, along with recommendations for DLNSEO, the LTCs, and IIE to consider as they continue to implement and grow the LTC Program.

Organization of This Report

The remainder of this report presents the results of our research. Chapter Two provides an overview of the LTC Program, including its history and a description of the organization and structure of the program today. Chapter Three discusses the objectives and goals of the LTC Program overall and as provided in documentation or articulated in interviews by representatives of the individual LTCs. Chapter Four provides information on instruction at the LTCs and how those who provide it are recruited, trained, supervised, and evaluated. Chapter Five discusses the various ways in which LTCs measure outcomes, including how performance is tracked at the IIE level and how LTCs rate their own progress and performance. Chapter Six examines aspects of the LTCs with respect to the community and collaboration. Chapter Seven discusses how LTCs use the funds awarded and what influences their utilization of those funds. Chapter Eight discusses the perceived and assessed advantages and disadvantages of LTCs operating within IHEs. Finally, Chapter Nine closes the report with conclusions and recommendations.

Appendix A provides the interview protocol for student interviews. Appendix B provides the interview protocol for teacher interviews. Appendix C provides the interview protocol for DoD partner interviews. Appendix D provides the interview protocol for LTC administrative interviews. Appendix E provides the interview protocol for DLNSEO leadership and staff interviews. Appendix F provides the interview protocol for IIE leadership and staff interviews. Appendix G provides the interview protocol for the cost interviews.

CHAPTER TWO

Overview of the Language Training Center Program

The LTC Program is an initiative under the National Security Education Program (NSEP) within DLNSEO. It is one of several initiatives designed to strengthen the language and cultural capabilities of the federal government, with a focus on national security. The LTC Program specifically "provides language and cultural training for DoD personnel by leveraging existing university programs to meet the needs of DoD organizations and units."[1] Since its beginning in 2011, the program has grown in the number of both centers and course offerings. As of the grant year that ended in 2017, the program included nine centers, which offer a variety of courses to meet the needs of their DoD partners. In this chapter, we provide a brief history of the LTC Program and how it fits into the overall portfolio of programs in NSEP. We then discuss the structure of the current program, including the range of courses offered and the manner in which they are designed. We also provide information on course delivery and venues for instruction gleaned from our interviews and site visits.

History of the Program

The LTC Program formally addresses the growing need for DoD personnel with expertise in critical languages and regional area skills. The LTC Program is part of a larger initiative within DoD to place a greater focus on language and cultural training. Since 2001, the Department has made strides to address this.

In its 2005 *Defense Language Transformation Roadmap*, DoD acknowledged that it needed to improve its capabilities in emerging critical languages and regional area skills.[2] This road map provides guidance on how to address the growing needs for language and regional expertise—skills that had previously not been emphasized as particularly important.

1 Language Training Center Program, "About LTC," webpage, undated (a).

2 Under Secretary of the Defense for Personnel and Readiness, *Defense Language Transformation Roadmap*, Washington, D.C.: U.S. Department of Defense, 2005.

In 2010, NSEP sponsored a congressionally requested report titled *Leveraging Language and Cultural Education and U.S. Higher Education Programs.*[3] That report, which was published in 2011, examined the potential to utilize the language and cultural programs at IHEs for national security purposes, and it encouraged DoD to take advantage of the existing language and cultural curricula at IHEs. The report references some existing relationships between the military and IHEs as examples of how DoD can benefit from such relationships. The 2011 report recommended that DoD "increase planning and support for coordinated strategic efforts with institutions of higher education to train DoD personnel."[4]

The NDAA for FY 2010 authorized DoD to establish LTCs at accredited IHEs.[5] The pilot for the LTCs began in 2011, through a collaboration between the Defense Language Office and NSEP.[6] The pilot program awarded one-year grants to five institutions. A new competition in 2012 awarded grants to the original five institutions and three additional institutions. According to DoD's October 2013 report to Congress, the LTC Program delivered 210 courses in its first two years, from the fall of 2011 through September 2013.[7] In 2013, a new three-year grant competition awarded grants to nine institutions. DoD recommended that the program continue for an additional three years, after which the program would be evaluated again. In 2015, the program added a new center in response to a service's request for additional focus on regional and area studies for foreign area officers as part of their professional development.[8] Another open competition for the LTCs was held in the winter of 2016, and eight institutions were awarded grants for the 2016–2017 fiscal year. Four centers have been a part of the program since the start, while some centers are new to the program. By the 2016–2017 grant year, the LTC Program had grown from five centers in 2011 to nine and offered more than 200 courses and provided training to more than 1,450 students in that year.[9]

---

3 Leah Mason and Bethany Haworth, *Leveraging Language and Cultural Education and U.S. Higher Education Programs*, New York: Institute of International Education, April 2011.

4 National Security Education Program. *2011 Annual Report*, Washington, D.C.: U.S. Department of Defense, 2011.

5 LTC Program, undated (b).

6 As explained in the next paragraph, the Defense Language Office was a predecessor to DLNSEO.

7 U.S. Department of Defense, 2013.

8 National Security Education Program, *2015 Annual Report*, Washington, D.C.: U.S. Department of Defense, 2015.

9 IIE, *Language Training Center Overview*, New York, 2017.

How the Program Fits into the Defense Language and National Security Education Office's Portfolio

DLNSEO has a diverse portfolio of initiatives that contribute to the mission of guiding DoD policy and planning for foreign-language, culture, and regional expertise.[10]

In 2012, NSEP merged with the Defense Language Office, forming DLNSEO. NSEP was originally created to forge a partnership between IHEs and the national security community. It has achieved this through initiatives that train the potential future national security workforce. There are currently nine initiatives, one of which is the LTC Program. All of the NSEP programs are designed to complement one another, so that the initiatives can learn and build off each other's work.

DLNSEO breaks its programs into five categories: K–12 enhancement, higher education, professional education, career enhancement, and surge capability. Although the LTC Program is considered professional education, the program is often compared to one of the higher education programs, Project Global Officer (Project GO). Project GO supports the language skills of future military officers in Reserve Officer Training Corps (ROTC) programs. Three universities in the LTC Program are also a part of Project GO. Representatives from DLNSEO and IIE noted that some of these other programs have more-obvious goals and objectives, and also have more collaborative communities, than the LTCs. However, the LTC Program is also one of the more recent additions to the portfolio, so it is still evolving.

The LTC Program was created to improve DoD's capabilities and expertise in strategic languages and regional studies. Through the partnerships formed between military units and IHEs, DoD sees the potential to increase the capacity for language instruction available to the Department and increase the range of instruction, including the availability of materials and actual instructors.

The program is administered by IIE, a not-for-profit organization that functions as DLNSEO's administrative partner to implement and oversee the LTC Program. IIE carries out an array of administrative processes, including issuing requests for proposals (RFPs), managing the proposal process, disbursing funds, and tracking LTC activities.

Structure of the Program Today

As of 2017, the LTC Program provides language and cultural training to military personnel through nine centers. These centers offer courses based on the needs of their respective DoD partners, with which they have forged formal relationships. Overall, the centers offer a wide variety of courses in a variety of ways on schedules that are designed to align with the needs of DoD partners to the greatest extent possible (while also working around potential conflicts with existing instruction at the institutions).

---

10 National Security Education Program, *2012 Annual Report*, Washington, D.C.: U.S. Department of Defense, 2012.

These courses include foreign-language training, training in culture and regional expertise, and professional writing courses for nonnative speakers of English. The centers implement varying methodologies for course design, delivery, and materials. The variations reflect the variation that is naturally occurring in the complex field of language instruction, as well as the variety of needs among DoD partners. For example, one LTC offers only foreign-language instruction in an iso-immersive setting (i.e., one in which the target language is spoken exclusively); another offers only writing courses via distance learning for speakers of English as a second language (ESL); another LTC offers only courses in regional studies. The other six LTCs offer foreign-language training, but they vary in the languages and levels that they offer, as well as in instructional methods. One of the LTCs provides much of its instruction via distance learning. Figure 2.1 reproduces a slide, provided to us by DLNSEO, that displays the LTCs in operation as of 2016, along with the languages taught and the DoD partners at the time. This same list continued through 2017 and 2018. Table 2.1 shows the courses offered at the nine LTCs currently in the program. The numbers following the language names refer to the proficiency levels targeted in the course.

Figure 2.1
List of LTCs, Languages Taught, and DoD Partners

LANGUAGE TRAINING CENTERS
ACADEMIC YEAR, 2016

UNIVERSITY/LANGUAGES	DoD PARTNER
California State University - Long Beach Arabic, Chinese, Persian (Farsi), French	California Army National Guard; 1st Radio Battalion; 351st Civil Affairs Command
Concordia College Arabic, Chinese, French, Korean, Russian	300th Military Intelligence Brigade
George Mason University (collaboration w/ University of Maryland-Baltimore County) English	National Security Agency
George Washington University FAO Regional Skill Sustainment Initiative	Navy/Service Foreign Area Officer (FAO) Proponent Office
North Carolina State University Arabic, Chinese, French, Korean, Portuguese, Spanish	JFK Special Warfare Center and School
San Diego State University Arabic, Georgian, Indonesian, Iraqi, Persian (Farsi), Pashto, Portuguese, Russian	1st Marine Division; Marine Corps Intelligence Support Battalion, 706th Military Intelligence Group
University of Kansas Arabic, French, German, Korean, Spanish, Japanese, Russian	Special Operations Forces (Command and General Staff Officers Course); Army National Guard; 10th Special Forces Group
University of Montana Arabic, Chinese, Indonesian, Korean, Pashto, Persian (Dari),	Special Operations Command; Army Special Operations Command; Marine Special Operations Command; 95th Civil Affairs Command; Military Information Support Operations Command
University of Utah Arabic, Chinese, French, Japanese, Persian (Farsi), Persian (Dari), Portuguese, Russian	300th Military Intelligence Brigade, 19th Special Forces Group; Utah National Guard; 169th Intelligence Squadron

SOURCE: Defense Language and National Security Education Office.

Table 2.1
Course Offerings in Language and Regional Expertise Across the LTC Program

Course	Concordia College	George Mason University	George Washington University	University of Utah	California State University–Long Beach	University of Kansas	University of Montana	North Carolina State University	San Diego State University	Total
ESL Writing		x								1
Regional Studies			x				x			2
Arabic 0–1	x					x		x		3
Arabic 1–1+	x					x	x	x		4
Arabic 2–3+	x					x				2
Arabic (Iraqi) 0–1									x	1
Arabic (Iraqi) 1–1+									x	1
Arabic (Iraqi) 2–3+									x	1
Arabic (Levantine) 0–1									x	1
Arabic (Levantine) 1–1+				x			x		x	3
Arabic (Levantine) 2–3+				x					x	2
Arabic (MSA) 0–1								x	x	2
Arabic (MSA) 1–1+				x	x		x	x		4

Table 2.1—Continued

Course	Concordia College	George Mason University	George Washington University	University of Utah	California State University–Long Beach	University of Kansas	University of Montana	North Carolina State University	San Diego State University	Total
Arabic (MSA) 2–3+				x	x					2
Chinese 0–1	x						x	x	x	4
Chinese 1–1+	x			x	x		x	x	x	6
Chinese 2–3+	x			x	x		x		x	5
French 0–1	x					x		x	x	4
French 1–1+	x			x	x	x		x	x	6
French 2–3+	x			x	x	x			x	5
German 0–1+						x				1
German 1–1+						x				1
German 2–3+						x				1
Georgian 0–1									x	1
Georgian 1–1+									x	1
Georgian 2–3+									x	1
Indonesian 0–1							x			1
Indonesian 1–1+							x			1
Indonesian 2–3+							x			1
Italian 0–1						x				1
Italian 1–1+						x				1

Table 2.1—Continued

Course	Concordia College	George Mason University	George Washington University	University of Utah	California State University–Long Beach	University of Kansas	University of Montana	North Carolina State University	San Diego State University	Total
Italian 2–3+						x				1
Japanese 0–1						x				1
Japanese 1–1+				x		x				2
Japanese 2–3+				x		x				2
Korean 0–1	x						x	x	x	4
Korean 1–1+	x			x			x	x	x	5
Korean 2–3+	x			x			x		x	4
Pashto 0–1									x	1
Pashto 1–1+									x	1
Pashto 2–3+									x	1
Persian 0–1						x				1
Persian 1–1+					x	x	x			3
Persian 2–3+					x	x				2
Persian (Dari) 0–1							x			1
Persian (Dari) 1–1+										0
Persian (Dari) 2–3+										0

Table 2.1—Continued

Course	Concordia College	George Mason University	George Washington University	University of Utah	California State University–Long Beach	University of Kansas	University of Montana	North Carolina State University	San Diego State University	Total
Persian (Farsi) 0–1	x								x	2
Persian (Farsi) 1–1+	x			x			x		x	4
Persian (Farsi) 2–3+	x			x					x	3
Portuguese 0–1	x							x		2
Portuguese 1–1+	x			x				x		3
Portuguese 2–3+	x			x						2
Russian 0–1	x					x		x	x	4
Russian 1–1+	x			x	x	x		x	x	6
Russian 2–3+	x			x	x	x			x	5
Spanish 0–1	x					x		x		3
Spanish 1–1+	x			x		x		x		4
Spanish 2–3+	x			x		x				3
Swahili 0–1									x	1
Swahili 1–1+									x	1
Swahili 2–3+									x	1

NOTES: In addition to the languages and topics shown in the table, in past years the program has also offered courses on Filipino (Tagalog), Turkish, Vietnamese, and Miskito. MSA = Modern Standard Arabic.

Course Offerings

In the 2016–2017 grant year, the LTC Program provided foreign-language training courses, regional training courses, and professional writing courses in English. Seven out of the nine centers provide foreign-language training; one provides regional expertise training; and one provides professional writing training in English for nonnative speakers. In the 2016–2017 fiscal year, more than 200 courses were offered in total, based on the information that the LTCs provided to our team. The largest number of courses offered by a single LTC was 77, and the smallest number was three. Five of the nine LTCs offered between five and 25 courses in one year. The median number of courses offered in that year was 15.

The languages taught in the 2016–2017 grant year were Arabic (Modern Standard Arabic [MSA], Levantine, and Iraqi), Chinese, Persian Dari and Farsi, French, ESL, German, Georgian, Korean, Italian, Japanese, Pashto, Portuguese, Russian, Spanish, Swahili, and Indonesian. The languages taught by the most LTCs were Arabic (seven LTCs), Chinese (six LTCs), French (six LTCs), and Russian (six LTCs).

As previously mentioned, one of the centers provides training only in regional expertise, not language. This center offers seven courses that provide relevant regional security training for specific commands, focusing on specific transregional topics. The center brings in experts on regional issues to present relevant material to the students. It primarily serves foreign area officers (FAOs) as part of their professional development. Another center reported that it incorporates short cultural trainings in addition to its language training.

The LTC Program uses the Interagency Language Roundtable (ILR) scale to describe the level of its trainings and student proficiencies.[11] This scale describes categories of language proficiency, from novice to functionally native, on a scale from 0 to 5. The centers that specialize in language training teach to a variety of levels, ranging from ILR 0 to 3+. One center provides beginner training focused on ILR 0 to 1+. Three centers provide training for all levels, ranging from ILR 0 to 3. Three LTCs provide language training primarily for intermediate and advanced levels from ILR 2 to 3+.

The LTCs offer many different types of courses, including intensive courses, tactical or initial acquisition training, professional training, intermediate and advanced courses, extension courses, refresher courses, and iso-immersion courses. Some centers focus on just one type of course, while others offer multiple.

According to the data provided by the LTCs, the duration of courses ranges from three to 150 days. For three centers, every course taught at their sites have the same duration. For the six other centers, the course length can vary depending on the partner and topic. The average course length for the 2016–2017 grant year ranged from

---

11 Interagency Language Roundtable, "Descriptions of Proficiency Levels," webpage, undated.

three to 60 days, with a mean of 22 days and a mode of 30. In hours, the length ranged from 20 to 360 hours, with a mean of 140 and a mode of 120.

Course Design

The LTCs use a variety of approaches to design their courses. Some centers have very structured curricula, whereas others are more fluid. In interviews, we asked center directors, staff, and instructors to tell us how they design their courses. They described various starting points, but all centers described a degree of flexibility to respond to the needs of the students.

Regarding the starting points for curriculum, two centers reported designing their courses based on materials used at the Defense Language Institute (DLI) Foreign Language Center. One LTC reported that it used its institution's existing language course curriculum and modified it to respond to the needs of its DoD partner. One LTC reported having its staff develop its curriculum with a subcontractor to assist in the curriculum development, assessments, and program evaluations.

Most LTCs reported that the instructors contribute substantially to the course design. One LTC begins the course design process by hosting a workshop for instructors at the beginning of every year to talk about overarching goals and needs and to share and collaborate on best practices. The LTC begins course planning by looking at the outcomes, then choosing the assessments, and finally designing learning interventions to move the course forward. Instructors meet with a technology and curriculum adviser who assists in the course design. Another LTC begins course planning with initial communication between instructors via email in the months and weeks leading up to the course. This could include instructors brainstorming a variety of topics that could be relevant for the course. The instructors then meet in person for three days before the course to collaborate and plan more thoroughly.

The LTC that offers regional training has a structured course design that centers on presentations by regional experts. The LTC finds experts who can address current events and issues that might be affecting commands and specific regions. Each of these courses also includes a simulation exercise focusing on a government response to a specific regional security challenge.

Some of the LTCs provided details on the daily structure of their courses. One LTC splits each day into a morning session focusing more on general language and cultural training and an afternoon session focusing on the operational needs of the students. Another LTC, which offers immersive training in language and culture, offers three to four hours of classroom-based language instruction along with six hours of cultural training, which includes meals, hands-on activities, and sports all conducted in the target language. Although this involves ten hours of formal interaction between students and instructors, there is informal interaction all hours of the day in this residential immersion program.

Several LTCs reported that they include cultural activities in their courses. As mentioned above, one LTC includes culturally appropriate meals and activities every day. Another LTC reported bringing speakers of the target language who live in the local area to speak to classes, and that LTC also conducts off-site field trips, including visits to culturally relevant sites in the local area, such as mosques and restaurants offering food associated with the culture and region of the target language.

Department of Defense Partner Input

Although all of the LTCs reported a strong desire to meet their DoD partners' needs, there was variation in the extent to which DoD partners communicated their needs. LTCs reported receiving varying amounts of information and guidance from their DoD partners regarding the needs of the students. Some LTCs reported that their DoD partners send data in advance on the students who will attend training at the LTC. These data can include prior test scores. However, these scores can be old and therefore not representative of the students' skill levels at the time they arrive for training. Some partners send students for training but do not ask for anything specific other than a certain language, leaving the LTC to assess the students on the first day of class and adjust the curriculum accordingly. One LTC reported sending course outlines to its partner prior to the course and receiving feedback. This LTC expressed that one of its partners (the DLI Foreign Language Center) is more involved than its other partners; other partners might convey very little about what they want students to learn. Another LTC was instructed by its partner to emphasize speaking, which the partner recognized to be a weakness of the students. A different DoD partner asked another LTC to provide more information about culture and the religions prevalent among speakers of the language to provide insight on topics that might not be a part of the training provided elsewhere. Overall, the interview data indicate that the degree of information provided by the DoD partners varies greatly, with some partners being very involved and others minimally so.

Materials

The LTCs use a variety of materials to aid instruction. Some use existing materials, some develop their own, and others do a combination of the two. Although a few LTCs use textbooks as a focus of instruction, many prefer to use original source material, such as target-language news and other media. A few LTCs currently use CL-150, a language learning platform from Transparent Language that allows an instructor to create a customized online "classroom." Through it, instructors can upload relevant information for their courses for students to access. Three LTCs reported using material from DLI. This includes DLI's Global Language Online Support System (GLOSS), an online system that offers written and audio material for many languages. One LTC mentioned that, because GLOSS does not cover all levels, the LTC has created lessons similar to those in the GLOSS style. And because many students attended

DLI previously, they are comfortable with GLOSS lessons. Three LTCs reported using online platforms, such as Canvas or Blackboard, to organize their material and make it accessible to the students.

Course Delivery

Delivery Methods

The LTC Program provides training through a variety of delivery methods. Seven of the nine LTCs deliver courses in person. Not all of the in-person courses are held at the actual universities. Only two LTCs deliver all of their courses entirely on the LTC's site. One of these is a residential immersion course. For six LTCs, instructors travel off-site to conduct courses, sometimes at the military installations where students are based. Two LTCs deliver training by distance learning. One of them delivers its courses entirely online, with no instructors physically in the same room with the students. This arrangement meets the DoD partner's need for information security due to the sensitive nature of their employees' work. The other offers instruction mainly through video teleconference (VTC). For this LTC, a resident instructor is present on-site with the students, and other instructors are based at the university. The distance options provide the students certain benefits, such as preservation of anonymity, which might be important for their jobs, and the ability to stay in the location at which they are based so they are still available for job responsibilities for part of the day.

Course Venues

Five LTCs have their own designated facilities at their affiliated institutions. One center has an academic resource center that provides technological and media support. It also has an extensive collection of language learning material that the center can utilize. This institution provides the LTC with access to three computer labs and a recording studio. Another LTC has a dedicated center with three classrooms and two language labs, and it has access to five additional university classrooms. This center also has a recording studio and web conference software. The LTC that offers instruction via VTC has 23 dedicated classrooms within its center, with similar equipment at the facilities of its partners. Another center has seven residential villages with authentic architecture and cultural décor. These isolated villages can also be adapted to serve other languages and cultures.

Conclusion

Since its inception in 2011, the LTC Program has expanded from five grant-funded centers to the nine that were in place in 2017. As allowed for in the design of the program, the current set of nine LTCs vary substantially. The array of options reflects the flexibility DLNSEO intended for meeting the varying needs for language and culture training within DoD. For example, some DoD partners need iso-immersion, whereas others prefer more traditional classroom instruction. The variety of ways in which courses are delivered also reflects a mix of traditional, classroom-based language and culture training with more innovative approaches, such as VTC delivery and in-residence immersion.

CHAPTER THREE

Language Training Center Objectives and Goals

The main objective of the LTCs is to provide language and culture training for DoD personnel. The legislation that authorizes the LTC Program breaks this down into specific objectives, and the DLNSEO, IIE, and LTC staffs interpret these objectives in the course of executing the program. To identify the explicit and implicit objectives of the program, we examined the legislation that authorized it, as well as LTC Program documents, and we interviewed staff members from DLNSEO, IIE, LTCs, and DoD partners. Then, to understand the extent to which the LTC Program and its centers were meeting the objectives, we compared the provided information with those objectives. We found that the LTC Program overall is meeting the objectives stated in the legislation and the objectives as they are interpreted by DLNSEO. In this chapter, we examine the program objectives codified in legislation and discuss objectives further defined in IIE, DLNSEO, and LTC Program documents and in interviews with leaders and staff. We then compare the LTC Program objectives currently in practice to the intended objectives stated in the authorizing legislation.

Objectives Stated in the Legislation and Program Documents

The LTC Program was officially authorized in Section 529 of the NDAA for FY 2010, which calls for the establishment of LTCs at IHEs. These centers are to serve members of the armed forces and civilian DoD employees in an effort to increase and improve capabilities in critical languages and regional skills. We provide the exact wording of the legislation below. It states that the LTC Program should include six elements:

1. Programs to provide that members of the Armed Forces or civilian employees of the Department of Defense who graduate from the institution of higher education concerned include members or employees, as the case may be, who are skilled in the languages and area studies covered by the program from beginning through advanced skills.

2. Programs of language proficiency training for such members and civilian employees at the institution of higher education concerned in critical and strategic languages tailored to meet operational readiness requirements.
3. Alternative language training delivery systems and modalities to meet language and regional area study requirements for such members and employees whether prior to deployment, during deployment, or post-deployment.
4. Programs on critical and strategic languages under the program that can be incorporated into the Reserve Officers' Training Corps programs to facilitate the development of language skills in such languages among future officers of the Armed Forces.
5. Training and education programs to expand the pool of qualified instructors and educators on critical and strategic languages and regional area studies under the program for the Armed Forces.
6. Programs to facilitate and encourage the recruitment of native and heritage speakers of critical and strategic languages under the program into the Armed Forces and the civilian workforce of the Department of Defense and to support the Civilian Linguist Reserve Corps.[1]

Judging by the data we collected on LTC Program activities, including course offerings and student data, the LTC Program has been successful in meeting the first five objectives stated in the legislation. We report the findings that support this conclusion in Chapter Two and elsewhere in the report, and we summarize them here as follows. For the first objective, we cite Table 2.1, which represents the breadth of language and area studies provided, covering beginning to advanced levels. For the second objective, we observed that the LTC Program provides training to DoD members and civilian employees in critical and strategic languages in response to the stated objectives of the DoD partners. While meeting operational readiness is a key element of the mandate, not knowing what the various operational readiness requirements are, we were unable to verify that the programs met them. The program providers relied on the DoD partners to ensure that their expressed requirements were designed to meet operational readiness requirements. For the third objective, the data reported in Chapter Two confirm that the LTCs employ "alternative language training delivery systems and modalities to meet language and area study requirements," as stated in the legislation. For the fourth objective, we note that three LTCs are situated at universities that are also part of Project GO, which serves members of the ROTC. These institutions leverage some of the same training resources to fulfill the needs of both programs. This demonstrates that the programs *can* be incorporated into ROTC programs as stated. For the fifth objective, we write in Chapter Four that a number of LTCs reported training instructors and providing them with professional development, which sug-

1 Public Law 111-84, 2009, Title IV, Military Personnel Policy, Subtitle C, Education and Training, Section 529, Language Training Centers for Members of the Armed Forces and Civilian Employees of the Department of Defense.

gests that they are expanding the pool of qualified instructors in the critical and strategic languages involved. However, the sixth objective, which focuses on the recruitment of native and heritage speakers, is difficult and perhaps not possible for the LTC Program to address directly, because there is little connection between the LTC's mandate to provide language training to service members and civilian employees and the ability to recruit for military or civilian service in the U.S. armed forces.

At the level of implementation, the LTC Program's RFP serves as an important document to communicate the program's goals to prospective institutions.[2] The RFP states the requirements and the expectations that applicants should plan to meet. This document states that the goal of the program is to "accelerate the development of foundational and higher level expertise in strategic languages and regional studies for DoD personnel by leveraging U.S. institutions of higher education to meet the existing and demonstrated training needs of DoD units, offices, or agencies." Again, based on the LTC course offerings and student data, the LTC Program has been meeting the stated objectives.

DLNSEO and IIE Objectives

In interviews, representatives from DLNSEO and IIE provided information regarding how they interpret and execute the objectives of the LTCs. DLNSEO representatives articulated the overarching objective of providing language and culture training for DoD personnel and doing so in a way that is flexible, agile, and responsive. They commented that the LTC Program differs from DLNSEO's other programs in not providing the same specific goals for all institutions carrying out the program. They also recognized that the goal of being flexible, agile, and responsive to the changing needs of DoD partners leads the various LTCs to have different individual goals depending on the needs of their DoD partners.

IIE, in its role as the administrative partner of DLNSEO, also plays a part in establishing and communicating LTC objectives, both directly and indirectly. One of IIE's responsibilities is to collect data on LTC performance regularly, which it does through a form known as the "assessment tracker." The assessment tracker collects data such as languages taught, number of hours of training, purpose of training, number of students trained, proficiency goal, and numbers of students tested. (See Table 5.1 in Chapter Five for a list of the data the assessment tracker collects.) The collection of these data represents an implicit message concerning the specific areas on which the LTCs should focus. The majority of fields in the assessment tracker focus on the provision of training—*x* subject for *y* days or weeks—rather than the outcomes of the

---

[2] Language Training Centers, "Request for Proposal: Language Training Center Program Sponsored by the Defense Language and National Security Education Office—Application Guidelines," 2016.

training—whether students increased their language proficiency or regional or cultural expertise as a result of the training and to what extent.

Language Training Center Objectives

Through interviews with LTC staff, we found that, in practice, the LTCs often create their own individual objectives within the main goals of the program. Some centers define their success in terms of whether their students meet proficiency goals, whereas others focus more on meeting the stated needs of their partners.

At least three centers specify proficiency goals. One LTC aims to increase language proficiency by a plus level on the ILR scale in at least one modality. Similarly, another center has an unwritten objective to raise students a plus level in one modality. One LTC focuses on reaching a minimum ILR level for all students. With defined proficiency goals, these LTCs have the ability to measure their success.

At least four centers did not articulate a specific objective apart from meeting the needs of its partners. One center emphasized that it is simply responsive to the needs of their partners, making it difficult to define one goal for the entire center. This center has several partners, and objectives vary by partner. Another center similarly stated that it has no overarching objective statement, because different partners have different needs. However, this LTC's staff members said that although they specialize in maintenance, they like to be able to see measurable increases in language proficiency. The partners articulate their needs in a variety of ways with varying degrees of specificity. For example, "provide training in *x* (language) for *y* (period of time)" and "provide initial (or maintenance) language training."

Two of the LTCs have specific purposes that differ from the others. One of these has an objective for ESL students to enhance professional writing and intercultural communication skills critical to DoD mission readiness. The other teaches regional expertise in the form of sustainment training in security issues. This LTC articulates targeted learning outcomes for each seminar. Even with these clearer missions, these objectives are not easily measurable.

DoD Partners' Objectives

The representatives of the DoD partners whom we interviewed also provided their interpretations of the objectives of the LTC Program. One saw the objective of the LTC Program as providing a certain type of training for a certain period of time. Another emphasized the importance of providing flexibility to existing instruction programs. For one partner, the LTC's goal was to provide a certain type of training, such as "initial" or "maintenance" language training. The DoD partners viewed the objectives of the LTC Program in terms of meeting their training needs, which they might interpret in terms of the actual type of training or the ability to adapt to their schedule.

Conclusion

The primary objectives of the LTC Program are articulated in the legislation that authorized the program and, in practice, trickle down through the ranks of those carrying out the program and those who hold a stake in it. We found that, overall, the LTC Program is meeting the goals stated in its authorizing legislation by providing training in language, culture, and regional expertise and enhancing the readiness of DoD personnel. Consistent with the legislation's focus on provision, many of those carrying out and taking advantage of the programs tended to focus simply on provision rather than on the outcomes of the programs.

With the LTC Program now well established in its eighth year of operation, there is an opportunity to strengthen the program and ensure its positive impact by increasing the focus on the outcomes of its training rather than merely on the provision of training. The LTC Program has demonstrated its ability to provide hundreds of courses per year to meet the needs of 24 DoD partners and more than 1,450 students in a single grant year.[3] A next step in the program's development could be for it to place further emphasis on the importance of successful training outcomes, work to arrive at appropriate ways to state specific center-level objectives, and measure the success in meeting them. We address this topic further in Chapter Five.

---

[3] IIE, 2017.

CHAPTER FOUR

Teachers: Recruiting, Training, and Evaluation

In education, it is widely accepted that teachers are the most important factor contributing to student achievement. Likewise, teachers play an important role within the LTC Program. Of all the LTC staff, they have the most direct contact with students by far, and they are the ones who actually provide the language and cultural training. With this in mind, we examined how teachers are recruited, hired, trained, and evaluated at the LTCs. From interviews with LTC directors, staff, and instructors, we found that centers use a variety of methods to do these things, and we describe those findings in this chapter.

Recruiting

Across the LTC Program, centers recruit teachers from within the affiliated university and from outside the university. Three LTCs reported that they recruit almost entirely from within the university, drawing from the university's language and cultural departments and other experts. Six LTCs recruit from both inside and outside the institution. These centers find teachers outside of the institution by utilizing known networks or open recruitment.

The LTCs that recruit from their affiliated universities reported that they recruit instructors from the already established language and cultural departments. One LTC selects program or language leaders from its pool of permanent or tenured faculty, recruiting specifically for faculty with experience in second-language acquisition or language pedagogy. It then relies on these individuals to select teachers for the courses. Some of these teachers may be current Ph.D. students or recent Ph.D. recipients. Another LTC reported recruiting native speakers from the university population.

The LTCs that also recruit from outside of the university reported that they search for teachers through networks or through open recruitment. One LTC reported that it relies exclusively on a network-based approach to find instructors. Another LTC reported that it utilizes the university's network to find candidates from media, nongovernmental organizations, religious groups, and the business sector. Yet another LTC reported that it draws on its wide network of previous faculty and students to find instructors. That LTC assigns a lead teacher for a course, and the lead teacher may use their own network to find additional instructors to assist. Within the instructional team for a course, this center aims to have some teachers who have taught at the center before and some who have not to encourage new ideas and practices.

Another LTC reported that it uses a combination of open job postings, social media, and word-of-mouth. Depending on the language, this LTC may first go through the university to see whether there are any available teachers or whether the departments have any recommendations. The LTC also seeks recommendations from past and present teachers and seeks to recruit teachers at conferences. Several of the teachers at this LTC reported learning about their positions from other teachers at the center.

One LTC reported following specific criteria when recruiting its lead teachers and teaching assistants. It reported requiring qualifications, such as assistant or associate professor experience, postsecondary education degrees, teaching experience, oral proficiency interview (OPI) certification, and in-country experience. The LTC also recruits scholars and graduate students from relevant countries, and the graduate teaching assistants are often screened and sponsored by the university.

Given the number and array of languages taught throughout the LTC Program, one might expect substantial challenges in recruiting teachers, but only two LTCs reported experiencing challenges in their teacher recruitment. One LTC reported occasional difficulties finding teachers for unexpected and short-notice requests from partners, which is to be expected. Another LTC reported having to release instructors because of cultural differences that affected the instructors' approach to teaching or ability to teach collaboratively within the LTC. For example, the LTC reported that one instructor did not want to work for a woman and another did not want to work with another instructor from a certain region.

Teacher Applicant Screening

Two LTCs described their screening processes in detail. For one LTC, the process begins with a résumé review of a potential instructor. LTC staff then interview the instructor and ask for a ten- to fifteen-minute lesson from candidates who show promise. After the lesson, the LTC provides feedback and sees how the candidate responds to the feedback. For this LTC, the candidate's response to feedback is at least as important as the quality of their teaching. Another LTC reported that it follows its IHE's hiring process and includes representatives from the DoD partner on the hiring committee for teachers.

Teacher Training

Several LTCs provide training opportunities for their instructors. Seven of the nine centers explicitly include training in their proposals. One LTC provides sponsorship for teachers to attend conferences and trainings. The instructors that we interviewed from this LTC reported feeling encouraged to take advantage of training opportunities. That LTC provides a weeklong training for teachers, in addition to OPI training. Teachers from this LTC also have the opportunity to observe other teachers' courses, and they are encouraged to provide feedback. Another LTC conducts a weeklong orientation program for new teachers. This includes a teaching demonstration, feedback, and an additional demonstration to determine whether feedback was utilized. If a teacher is found to need additional training, the LTC provides a training plan. The LTC also provides CL-150 training and OPI tester training and certification through the American Council on the Teaching of Foreign Languages (ACTFL). Another LTC also provides professional development opportunities, by providing instructors training on administering the ACTFL and OPI tests. One LTC provides training for new instructors and offers ongoing training for all instructors through workshops each semester. Another LTC provides a two-day instructional leadership training for its lead teachers. Teachers at this LTC reported that the LTC staff were responsive to their requests for professional learning. One told an anecdote about asking for more information on the ILR scale and being given the opportunity to speak with a representative from ILR, which the teachers found beneficial.

Teacher Staffing

The number of instructors and teaching assistants supporting a course varies across LTCs and courses. Two LTCs reported that they typically assign one instructor per course. For the LTCs that offer different types of courses with different partners, the number of instructors and teaching assistants varies accordingly. For language courses, the maximum instructor-to-student ratio is 1:10, and the minimum is 1:3. Six of the nine courses use teaching assistants in addition to the instructors. For one center, a teaching assistant may be assigned if the class size exceeds the typical ratio of instructors to students. The center that utilizes VTC typically has one instructor assisting on site at the military installation, a head instructor based at the university, and two to three graduate teaching assistants to offer additional instruction. The center that offers regional expertise training typically has 12 speakers per course.

Teacher Evaluation

The LTCs use a variety of methods to evaluate the performance and quality of instructors, as represented in Table 4.1. Seven of the nine LTCs use classroom observations, some being formal observations, others being more informal. One of these LTCs reported that it always does two classroom observations during a course to determine whether the teacher implemented feedback from the first. One LTC reported having teaching peers conduct observations and complete rubrics to provide feedback. Two LTCs reported that they consider course outcomes when evaluating teacher performance. One LTC reported that it requests biweekly reports from teachers. Every LTC reported using course evaluations by students to gain insight on the quality of instruction. One LTC reported conducting preliminary evaluations with students after the first week of a course to determine whether improvements need to be made for the subsequent weeks.

Observations on LTC Teachers and Instruction

Judging from our interviews with LTC directors, students, instructors, and DoD partners, teaching appears to be strong throughout the program. LTC directors all spoke highly of their teachers. The students and DoD partners generally expressed satisfaction with the quality of instruction. Most of the instructors we interviewed also reported that they enjoy teaching for the LTCs.

Along with these positive observations, some challenges also surfaced. Many instructors commented on the need to create their own materials because of limited

Table 4.1
Methods of Teacher Evaluation

	Class Observations	Outcomes	Instructor Reports	Course Evaluations	Interim Feedback	Team Meetings
LTC 1	√			√		√
LTC 2				√		
LTC 3				√		
LTC 4	√			√		
LTC 5				√		
LTC 6	√	√	√	√		
LTC 7	√	√		√		
LTC 8	√			√	√	√
LTC 9	√			√		

availability of teaching materials in certain less commonly taught languages. We also noted that some centers and instructors were reluctant to share information with other LTCs. Some instructors expressed surprise that there are other instructors across the program teaching similar courses and creating their own materials. These observations suggest an opportunity for greater collaboration among the centers.

Conclusion

Teachers are crucially important to the LTCs, and the teaching is regarded as strong by LTC directors, the students we met at site visits, and DoD partners. It was beyond the scope of this study to evaluate LTC teaching quality directly. Contrary to expectations, few LTCs reported substantial difficulties recruiting teachers, which may reflect one of the advantages of their relationships with IHEs and their networks. However, we found that LTCs vary widely in how they train and evaluate their instructors, which suggests that a variety of standards and expectations are being applied when thinking about the quality of teaching. We also heard from a number of teachers that they feel the need to develop their own materials, and some others expressed a reluctance to share information with other teachers or other LTCs.

These last three observations point the way to opportunities for growth. In interviews and unstructured discussions with LTC directors and staff, many expressed an interest in learning more about other LTCs' practices. Relevant to teachers and their training, the LTC Program may benefit from establishing some program-wide professional development opportunities that bring together teachers and instructional leaders from across the LTC Program. Such actions may begin to foster common approaches to training and evaluation where appropriate, and they may also lay a foundation for collaboration across the LTCs. If successful, over time, this could lead to more sharing of methods and materials across LTCs and strengthen feelings of being part of an LTC professional community.

CHAPTER FIVE

Measuring Outcomes

Measuring outcomes in student performance helps guide future learning for the student and can help guide educational institutions to improve their programs. We examined outcome measurement at each of the nine LTCs by eliciting descriptions of their measurement practices, interviewing instructors and staff, and examining their measurement data when available. This chapter will discuss the results of that examination, explain how different methods and standards for measurement are used, and discuss potential improvements to measurement within the LTC Program overall.

Tracking Student Performance

Processes and procedures for measuring student performance vary widely across the LTCs. For programs that conduct intermediate language instruction, pre-testing is common but not the rule. Some LTCs use the student's last recorded Defense Language Proficiency Test (DLPT) score to make a general determination of the student's language ability. Others rely on the sponsor language program manager or CLPM to place students into classes according to ILR scores from the most recent DLPT. While both of these methods may provide some level of confidence in the student's correct placement, they are also often inaccurate, according to interviews with teachers, LTC staff, and students themselves. DLPT scores may be old or outdated, or the student may not have tested well on the day of the DLPT.

LTCs and student interviews revealed multiple instances each year when teacher assessments of a student's ability or student requests for an in-progress class change resulted in moving a student to a lower or higher level group, if one was available. This is not necessarily a negative, as it suggests that LTC faculty members adjust accordingly when they observe students who overperform or underperform the group norm, and many students feel comfortable discussing their language learning needs with instructors and LTC Program managers. The flexibility to move students from one group to another is one of the strengths of the LTC language programs, although this flexibility is not available for every language taught at every LTC. (See Chapter Six for instructors' perspectives on this topic.)

Five of seven LTCs that teach intermediate-level foreign languages administer a pre-test that assists faculty in identifying individual student strengths and weaknesses. The pre-test is also useful to assist instructors with designing or revising course curriculum as required. Assessment instruments across the LTCs that use them vary widely and include OPI, the American Council of Teachers of Foreign Languages–Listening Proficiency Test (ACTFL LPT), and the American Council of Teachers of Foreign Languages–Reading Proficiency Test (ACTFL RPT).

Even though there are similarities among many of the courses taught across the LTCs, there is little similarity in the minimum program goals that each LTC is aspiring to reach or maintain with each course. Sponsor expectations for many LTCs were phrased using "provision of training" language; for example, teach Farsi for six weeks, or provide regional orientation, without any specific measurable outcome goals indicated. As a result, LTC goals for student outcomes varied significantly across programs, as did actual student outcomes. For example, LTC Program explanations of goals for student outcomes on LTC language courses included the following broad spectrum of expected results:

- "improvement in 55 percent of our students"
- 60–70 percent improve by a "plus" (i.e., half level) on the ILR scale
- 70 percent to the "next level" on OPI
- 80 percent of students "sustain or improve" by end of course
- 95 percent improve to a 1 on the DLPT.

Tracking Language Training Center Performance

There are multiple different mechanisms used to track the performance of the LTC. At the programmatic level, each LTC is required to complete the *assessment tracker*, which is an Excel workbook created by IIE to collect data on each program. LTCs also complete quarterly and final reviews to provide additional information to IIE. On an individual level, the LTCs monitor their own performance frequently through course evaluations and student surveys that provide more-detailed feedback on course quality and student satisfaction.

Assessment Tracker

IIE developed the assessment tracker in 2012 to collect data across the LTC program to assist in reporting, taking into account DLNSEO's need to report to Congress. Each center completes the assessment tracker to report data on the courses it offers and the proficiency outcomes of students, if measured. The current version of the tracker includes fields for available numeric, categorical, and qualitative data for every course offered by an LTC. Data collected include the fields indicated in Table 5.1.

Table 5.1
Data and Data Types Collected in the Assessment Tracker

Data Field	Field Type	Options for Categorical Responses
Name of Course	Open response	
Start Date	Quantitative	
End Date	Quantitative	
Training Days	Quantitative	
Contact Hours	Quantitative	
Course Category	Categorical	Culture and Language, Language, Regional Studies
Language	Categorical	Arabic, Arabic (Levantine), Arabic (Iraqi), Arabic (Yemeni), Chinese, Dari, English, French, French (African), Georgian, German, Hebrew, Hindi, Indonesian, Italian, Japanese, Korean, Miskito, Mixtec, Pashto, Persian, Portuguese, Russian, Spanish, Swahili, Tagalog, Thai, Turkic, Turkish, Urdu, Uzbek, Wolof, Zapotec, N/A
Course Level	Categorical	Novice, Intermediate, Advanced, Superior
Course Description	Open response	
Course Delivery	Categorical	Asynchronous, Blended, Classroom, Synchronous
Number of Students	Quantitative	
Purpose of Training	Categorical	Enhancement, Conversion, Initial Acquisition, Iso-Immersion, Sustainment, Other
Other (Purpose of Training)	Open response	
Professional Goal	Categorical	FAO Training, Language Billet, Pre-Deployment, Regional Affiliation, State Partnership, Other
Other (Professional Goal)	Open response	
Single Training or Part of Series	Categorical	Single Training, Part of a Series
Series Identification	Open Response	
DoD Partner	Open response	
Component	Categorical	Active Duty, DoD Civilian, Guard/Reserve, Other/combined category
Service	Categorical	Air Force, Army, Marine Corps, Navy, Combined, Other
Other (Service)	Open response	

Table 5.1—Continued

Data Field	Field Type	Options for Categorical Responses
Assessment Tool	Categorical	ACTFL, BYU Adaptive Reading/Listening, CL-150, DLPT, Flagship Online Reading/Listening Test, OPI, Service Academy Test, STAMP
Proficiency Goal	Categorical	ILR 0, ILR 0+, ILR 1, ILR 1+, ILR 2, ILR 2+, ILR 3, ILR 3+, ILR 4, ILR 4+, ILR 5, ACTFL Novice Low, ACTFL Novice Medium, ACTFL Novice High, ACTFL Intermediate Low, ACTFL Intermediate Medium, ACTFL Intermediate High, ACTFL Advanced Low, ACTFL Advanced Medium, ACTFL Advanced High, ACTFL Superior, Plus Level Increase, Sublevel Increase, Threshold Increase
Proficiency Goal Notes	Open response	
Number of Students Tested	Quantitative	
Number of Students That Met or Exceeded Goals	Quantitative	
Number of Students per Outcome Measurement	Quantitative	
Comments	Open response	

NOTE: A categorical field is one in which the respondent selects from a list of possible answers provided on the survey instrument. BYU = Brigham Young University; STAMP = Standards-Based Measurement of Proficiency.

IIE staff reported that the assessment tracker has evolved since its first iteration, with adjustments made to provide clearer data to IIE and to incorporate feedback gathered from the centers. While the context requested has mainly stayed the same, data fields have been clarified to provide better guidance to the centers for their use when they fill out the tracker. For example, changes were made to allow input of data that better indicate what LTCs actually are doing (the purpose of training) and to get more-precise data for reporting purposes, such as percentage of students meeting program goals.[1] Also, changes have been made to account for new course offerings that are particularly unique. For example, IIE added "Regional Studies" to the drop-down menu for Course Categories, because a center began offering regional studies courses that did not fall into the "Culture and Language" or "Language" category. There has also been some reorganization of the information to improve the continuity of the data. IIE has consulted with the centers about the assessment tracker and has made changes based on this feedback.

1 Email communication from IIE staff, February 2018.

Representatives from DLNSEO and IIE provided candid feedback on the content and utility of the assessment tracker. There was a general consensus that the tracker provides good data on proficiency gains and student enrollment of the language training centers, but at least one person interviewed noted that while the assessment tracker collects the numbers of students and numbers of languages offered, it does not collect information on the quality of the training, although the interviewee did not state specifically what that would entail. Several interviewees felt that IIE should develop better metrics to measure the LTCs, noting that there could be important qualitative information that is not captured by the current version of the assessment tracker. At least one interviewee suggested that the data collected in the assessment tracker could be better utilized for purposes of research and analysis. IIE staff admitted that they had not yet fully exploited the data collected to derive insights about the LTC Program.

LTC administrators and staff also shared their impressions of the assessment tracker. Two LTCs suggested that the format of the assessment tracker could be improved from its current spreadsheet format, which works similarly to a Word document, to a more interactive dataset. Interviewees noted that there is some redundancy of information requested in both the assessment tracker and the quarterly and final reports required by IIE and DLNSEO. One interviewee commented that the assessment tracker does not fit within a standard computer screen very well, which makes it somewhat challenging to complete. More than one LTC suggested that the assessment tracker is tedious and not very user-friendly.

Multiple LTCs indicated concerns not just with the format but also with the content collected and maintained in the assessment tracker. One LTC commented that the assessment tracker does not fully capture what the LTCs offer or provide to their students. The assessment tracker is focused on assessments and meeting proficiency goals, but some centers, according to several interviewees, offer and specialize in sustainment training that may not result in obvious proficiency gains. Because of the DLPT testing process, it is challenging for many LTCs to show improvement in students. At least one interviewee suggested that this disconnect in the way goals are captured might lead some LTCs to misrepresent their progress on the assessment tracker.

One data field considered missing from the assessment tracker is incoming test or pre-test score. The tracker currently only has a field for outgoing proficiency scores, even though it might be useful to be able to show comparative scores to sponsors or to report to IIE and DLNSEO through the tracker. Interviewees suggested that it could also be helpful to include the date of the incoming test scores, because some students come into the courses with outdated DLPT scores that are no longer representative of their current skill level.

Course Evaluation Methods Used by the Language Training Centers

LTCs each have their own methods for evaluating their successes and achievements. Every LTC reported administering end-of-course evaluations and student surveys to gather feedback on their courses. These evaluations focus on the perspectives of the students and provide information on the quality of the courses but varied in length from seven to 94 questions. LTCs value the feedback received from course evaluations, as more is revealed about the quality of the course and student satisfaction from detailed evaluations than from proficiency scores. Wide disparity in the evaluation questions and responses across LTCs, however, makes it difficult to compare and contrast even similar LTCs using available data.

During our study, we had access to course evaluations from seven LTCs. Their length and composition varied widely.

One evaluation was entirely composed of open-response questions, but most included a mix of Likert-scale questions and open-response questions.[2] The content of the evaluations also varied widely by center. One center asked particularly detailed questions about the students' learning style and motivations. Another center asked several questions about the materials and exercises that had been used in the course. While some centers asked very specific questions about the instruction and materials, others were relatively simple, asking just a few questions on the quality of the course, instructors, and educational materials.

Despite each school having a unique course evaluation method, some commonality exists among the seven evaluations we saw. All seven LTCs asked students questions about the positive and negative aspects of the course or the instructor, such as "What did you like most/least about this course and/or the instructor? Please give examples" and "What types of activities do you enjoy learning from the most/least?" Four of the seven LTC evaluations included a space for additional comments or suggestions for improvements, and a separate set of four LTCs asked students to provide information or ratings on the quality of the instructors and speakers. The commonalities across the evaluations all focused on gathering information about the quality of the course and the satisfaction of the students.

Some LTCs discussed how they utilize their course evaluations in detail. One LTC focuses on gaining information about the motivation of students. While the LTC does not want to make the course evaluation too burdensome for the student, it is very interested in collecting data to find out what parts of the program have the most positive impact on students. While this LTC used to have one standard evaluation for all courses, it now uses a few different versions to account for different types of methodologies used in courses.

---

2 Likert-scale response options varied from test to test; some used "not at all" to "extremely," whereas others used "excellent" to "poor." This variation in type of response received makes it difficult to compare across courses.

Conclusion

DLNSEO, IIE, and the individual LTCs recognize the importance of measuring outcomes and tracking performance of the centers, but they all do it in different ways. The assessment tracker used by IIE and DLNSEO focuses on proficiency gains and enrollment and does not collect data on the quality of the course or satisfaction of the students. While this provides information on the impact of the LTCs, it does not give any information on the quality of education being provided. As noted by both IIE and DLNSEO representatives and individual LTC administrators, the assessment tracker does not capture some of the more nuanced aspects of LTCs. The format of the assessment tracker and the process in combination with quarterly reports can also be tedious for the LTCs. However, the assessment tracker does allow IIE and DLNSEO to keep records of how many students, courses, and types of courses are offered throughout the entire program.

Many of the individual centers collect data on how the students perceived the course and what aspects were liked and disliked. Through this, the individual LTCs are made aware of challenges and successes and can perhaps adapt their courses as needed. While many LTCs recognize the importance of collecting this type of data, the range of questions asked varies greatly. This is partly because the types of courses and the styles of courses vary greatly, both across the LTCs as a whole and even within individual LTCs. However, even with the differences, based on the sample of evaluations that we had access to, the LTCs do try to use the course evaluations to gather information on the quality of the courses. IIE could work to make improvements to the assessment tracker so that entering, manipulating, and using data would be easier and more intuitive for all involved.

Given the variety in courses, students, and DoD partner needs, it is not surprising that there is variation in approaches to measurement across the program. The LTCs vary in the languages they teach (and they do not all teach languages), the levels of proficiency they target, the purposes of their training, and the DoD partners they serve. We do not suggest setting requirements for specific student assessments to be applied across the program (which would be impossible to implement in practice). A more feasible approach may be to encourage each LTC to articulate objectives that go beyond provision and represent meaningful training outcomes for the DoD partners and students. This process could be done initially through a pilot phase dedicated to identifying appropriate, meaningful, and measurable outcomes for the respective centers. Following the pilot phase, reporting such measures of success could become a requirement stated in the RFP and implemented through the course of normal program activities. Furthermore, to measure LTC performance outside of student outcomes, DLNSEO and IIE could create a standardized survey on the quality of instruction at the LTCs or establish a small set of questions for each site to include in its feedback survey. This would enable the creation of data that could be analyzed across the LTC Program.

Finally, where similar courses are taught across LTCs, DLNSEO, IIE, and the LTCs together could agree on minimum program goals according to course, language, level, purpose, length, and sponsor criteria to ensure consistency of outcomes across the LTC Program.

CHAPTER SIX

Professional Community and Collaboration

As a part of our study, we interviewed a range of stakeholders of the program to gain insights on aspects of community and collaboration. In addition to interviewing the administrative staff from each LTC, we interviewed students and instructors at several of the LTCs. We also spoke to ten command language program managers (CLPMs) and senior language authorities (SLAs) from the DoD organizations that partner with the LTCs. Interviews helped us gain an understanding of the roles of each stakeholder in the LTC Program and how they interact and communicate with one another. In this chapter, we discuss our observations on the relationships and perceptions of relationships that exist among the stakeholders we interviewed, offer some suggestions for improving communications and collaboration, and suggest the possibility of identifying and implementing overall program synergies.

Language Training Center Directors and Staff

The administrative staff from each LTC provided us with their perspectives on the program, highlighting benefits and challenges and offering recommendations that could potentially improve the program in the future.

Benefits

LTC directors and staff unanimously conveyed high levels of commitment and engagement toward the program. Several LTCs noted that the program benefits both the university and the students, providing new teaching challenges and opportunities to the university while offering academically rich programs to students. One LTC noted that the program promotes a valuable cultural exchange between people with academic backgrounds and military personnel, and another suggested that being at a university may spark students' interest in pursuing higher education beyond the duration of the LTC course in question. That LTC shared an anecdote of a student who became interested in pursuing higher education because of his positive experience at the LTC.

Challenges

LTC staff also pointed out some challenges they face as a part of the program. A few LTCs suggested that better communication with their DoD partners would enhance their ability to fill seats, provide quality instruction, and adjust curriculum and content in a more responsive manner. Two LTCs noted that communication with their DoD partners had been particularly challenging, and, as a result, they did not have a full understanding of demand signals and mission needs. One LTC expressed a concern that its staff had to devote too much time to marketing itself to potential partners, and at least three LTCs stated that they would like to have more communication with the partners that they already have. One LTC noted that a greater understanding of its partner's needs would allow the center to better tailor the courses to the students.

Two LTCs described a sense of competition amongst the LTCs, which they felt might be harmful to the mission success of the centers. Knowing that DLNSEO has a specific amount of funds to distribute among the LTCs, some LTC directors perceive a zero-sum situation. Furthermore, some LTCs have concerns about competing for DoD partners. One LTC pointed out that several centers are catering to the same audience by offering similarly higher-level language training, leading to competition for DoD partners. Another LTC commented that having to compete for funding may cause centers to focus on training that may be outside of their expertise, as they may add training that they would not otherwise attempt to provide in order to enlarge their portfolios. Although DLNSEO and IIE conveyed that they do not wish the LTCs to be in competition with one another, comments from some LTCs suggest an undercurrent of competition.

Recommendations

The LTCs also offered some recommendations for change, enhancement, or improvement of the LTC Program. Two LTCs asked for more-centralized professional development opportunities for instructors. Two LTCs suggested that communication among LTCs and between LTCs and DLNSEO is too infrequent and suggested that there be more than one LTC-wide meeting each year. Also suggested was that annual meetings be hosted at actual LTCs on a rotating basis, rather than in Washington, D.C., so that LTCs could get a better understanding of each other's circumstances, course offerings, and challenges. One LTC suggested that DLNSEO begin documenting promising practices among the LTCs, and another suggested that the centers could benefit from a glossary of military terminology. Several LTCs expressed interest in learning more about the other centers. The centers also showed interest in more information-sharing among the centers to foster a more collaborative program.

Instructors' Perspectives

We spoke to instructors at six of the nine LTCs. The instructors provided information on their experiences working at the LTCs and their interactions with students. They provided insights on the program as a whole, along with further information about their teaching styles and interactions with students.

Positives

All of the instructors we met with expressed positive sentiments about their work and a strong commitment to effective teaching. Instructors at four of the LTCs reported that their students are very motivated and focused. At one LTC, the instructors reported that they wanted specifically to teach within the LTC because they enjoy the experience so much. Most of the instructors with whom we spoke also expressed satisfaction with the LTC management. Several instructors conveyed that they feel very supported by the LTC management, and instructors with at least one LTC noted that the management was very encouraging of professional development opportunities. One instructor told an anecdote about their LTC's management arranging a meeting with a representative from ILR because an instructor expressed interest in learning more about the ILR language proficiency scale. Several instructors stated that they wish they could teach more courses at the LTCs.

Challenges

Instructors also reported some challenges associated with teaching for an LTC. Instructors from two centers expressed the opinion that their students are generally "too focused" on test scores. Those instructors commented that they would like the students to focus more on the overall development of their language skills, rather than just on the test. Instructors at another LTC commented that their students seemed to want to memorize answers for the OPI.

Several instructors stated that they would like to have more information regarding the needs and the mission of the students. The instructors at one center expressed an interest in visiting DLI to have a better understanding of the setting in which students first learned their language. A few instructors also mentioned that assessing the proficiency levels of incoming students can be challenging. They reported that students are often sent to training based on their last test scores, but the test scores may be old and no longer indicative of a student's current skills. Instructors also reported sometimes having a wide range of proficiency levels in a single class, which is challenging. They reported that they do not always have the ability to move students to a higher or lower level group. Some reported that they address the challenge by providing more individual attention, such as tutoring, to students to help them advance more quickly if they are at a lower level or to provide more challenge to students if they are at a higher level.

At one center, where instructors were teaching a two-week intensive course, the instructors commented on the challenges they associated with part-time teaching. Even though the particular language had been taught before at the LTC, the instructors reported that none of the previous instructors had returned and that the new instructors had to build curriculum from scratch. The instructors pointed out the importance of institutional memory and expressed a hope that the center could implement measures to reduce staff turnover. Instructors suggested that if the program is going to grow, centers like theirs should invest in full-time instructors.

DoD Partners' Perspectives

We spoke with several CLPMs and SLAs who represent the military units and DoD organizations that partner with the LTCs. These interviewees described their relationships with the LTCs, expressed satisfaction with the quality and value of the instruction provided, and praised the flexibility of the program overall and the LTCs in particular.

Two CLPMs described how they determine which service members in their organizations will receive training. One CLPM sends its service members a catalogue of all the available courses in advance of course offerings, then administers a survey to determine who would like to attend language training. The CLPM then groups students by language and level and sends the information to the LTC. Another CLPM explained that the unit advertises the courses in advance, and students may choose to attend if the course fits into their schedules. Some CLPMs reported that representatives from their LTC have given briefings to potential students as a way of improving communication and increasing interest in the courses.

During the CLPM and SLA interviews we conducted, we observed a range of levels of interaction with LTCs, running from nearly continuous to infrequent. Several CLPMs and SLAs indicated that they have regular communications with the LTC, talking with LTC leadership or staff before every course and exchanging major updates at the beginning of every program year. One CLPM described "regular communication" with the LTC in the form of as-needed email and phone conversations. One CLPM, who was relatively new to the job, had not had frequent communication with the LTC but was aware of whom to contact if required.

The CLPMs and SLAs with whom we spoke expressed nothing but support for the program overall and their LTC in particular. All of those we spoke with suggested that their LTCs were meeting their training needs. CLPMs described the services of the LTC as "mission critical" and "central to our success." One CLPM suggested that their LTC was "a key component of [their] overall program," and another stated that "language is an important component for all our missions. We need this." Flexibility in the program was commented on by multiple CLPMs and SLAs as a strength, and two CLPMs emphasized that the LTCs are "very flexible" and responsive to their needs.

Several CLPMs emphasized responsiveness as a key characteristic of their LTC: "They give us everything we ask for." One CLPM noted that while their LTC works hard to be flexible and responsive, it can be challenging to coordinate schedules, because mission calendars, program year, and academic years are not always synchronized. Some CLPMs commented that many LTC instructors appear to want to take summers off, but summer is often the most convenient time for some units to participate in specialized training. However, this scheduling challenge was not true of all LTCs; we note in Chapter Eight that at least one LTC has its greatest capacity during the summer, when its instructors are free from their school-year responsibilities.

At one LTC, space is at a premium, which was not only observed by the research team but also commented on by the CLPM. Students returning from training at that LTC were pleased with the level of instruction but often commented on the lack of dedicated space for classwork and seminars.

One CLPM whose organization trains a large number of linguists through multiple training means suggested that it is beneficial to the learning process and for student well-being for language instruction to be separated from the military environment. The CLPM expressed the view that when students are away from the military base, they feel like they are having a break even though they are working hard, and they are not distracted by all the tasks and duties that accompany life in the military.

Overall, the DoD partners seemed highly satisfied with the LTC Program and with their relationships with the LTCs. Several suggested that the only thing that could improve the LTC Program was having more of it: more courses, more opportunities, and more resources.

Student Perspectives

We met with students from six of the nine LTCs, and they reported varying motivations for attending courses, ranging from "checking the box" and mandatory requirement, to mission-critical skills training and deep personal interest. The students also expressed a range of levels of engagement and satisfaction with the course. While many students expected to utilize their language skills on the job, many did not, either because they thought it unlikely that they would use the specific language they were learning in their future work or because they did not expect their specific mission requirements to require them to use a foreign language. Regardless of the motivation levels of students, they generally seemed satisfied with the quality of instruction at the LTCs. Some students, both career linguists and those who had mission changes that caused them to learn a new language, expressed the opinion that the LTC Program was the best language training they had encountered while in service.

Attending a Language Training Center

Students described the process and motivation for attending training at an LTC. Most students were attending a course either for a periodic or annual language training requirement, to prepare for deployment, or to assist in meeting a language level (ILR proficiency) requirement for their job. Students from one unit described having seen a catalogue of courses sent by the CLPM and being asked to pick the courses in which they are interested. Others described being directed or "voluntold" to attend the course to meet an annual requirement.

The students described different processes for being sent to training at an LTC. At one center, we met with students who were receiving training to prepare for deployment. Some of those students reported that they had been selected by their unit to attend, whereas others reported having specifically asked to attend. The students at one center reported that they were all attending the course to meet a certain level requirement for their job. At another center, all the students reported that they had volunteered to attend the course as a part of their yearly training to refresh their language skills. In a very small number of cases, students reported not attending the specific training they desired. One student planned to attend a course for a different language but ended up in a different course because of a scheduling problem. Another student reported choosing a course not because it was his first choice, but because it worked best in his schedule. In general, the students we spoke with reported being satisfied with the level of instruction, and many described the training as better than the language training they had received elsewhere.

Engagement of Students

During site visits, we observed that the level of engagement of the students varied. At two centers, we observed a very high level of engagement among the students, who appeared to greatly enjoy the courses and who commented positively about their value. One of these centers offered a uniquely immersive, in-residence experience. The students at that site reported that they found the immersive experience to be more conducive to learning than other language training they had attended. The other center also offered an in-residence experience. The students at that site reported that they perceived it as an honor to be able attend the course and that they enjoyed being on the institution's campus. They commented that being away from the military base and its culture put them in a better mindset for learning and that it allowed them to focus exclusively on their language training. At another center, we observed mixed levels of student engagement; however, most students at that site reported being satisfied with the course and that it met their needs. Those students commented that they appreciated the level of instruction and the professionalism of the instructors. At one LTC, some of the students expressed disappointment at the pace of their course, commenting that it moved slowly and was not as challenging as they had expected. Some students who commuted to and from an LTC each day reported that they found the course's start time in the middle of the day to be challenging and that they commuted for more than an hour each way. One center taught via distance learning, and some students in that LTC's courses commented that the training might benefit them more if it they could attend away from their base.

Application of Skills

Some students reported that they expected to apply their new skills to their jobs more than others. The students who reported that they were preparing to deploy generally also reported that they expected to use their new skills on the job immediately. At one center, students who were not expecting to deploy in the immediate future noted that while not all of them actively used the language on the job, they needed to be prepared. These students could be switched with little warning to a unit that would require them to use the language immediately. However, some students reported little to no expectation of needing to use their language skills in their jobs, unless there was a major change in circumstances affecting national security that related to their language. In one course, none of the students reported expecting to be sent to a place where they would use their language. Such comments do not reflect on the quality of instruction, but rather on other circumstances that are beyond the control of LTCs.

Conclusion

The LTC Program brings together military personnel and representatives from IHEs. This results in unique and valuable experiences for both. The instructors and LTC administrative staff conveyed high levels of commitment to their work and appeared to find the experience rewarding. The DoD partners expressed satisfaction with the LTC Program and praised the responsiveness of the LTCs. The engagement of students varied greatly, but most students felt that the courses were meeting their needs, and some expressed the opinion that the quality of the training they received at the LTC they attended was superior to what they had experienced elsewhere.

The relationships between the LTCs and their DoD stakeholders appear to be generally positive. However, there are opportunities to strengthen communication between the LTCs and their DoD partners. Greater communication could increase attendance and provide information to instructors to further tailor the courses to the students' needs.

The sense of competition among the LTCs poses a challenge to the program as a whole. The LTC Program could benefit from fostering a culture of collaboration among the LTCs. Although it is not always productive to require collaboration by mandate, DLNSEO could take steps to encourage a culture of collaboration among the current LTCs and consider adding collaboration as an expectation in the RFP in the future to reduce competition and enhance synergies. Additionally, the LTC Program could solicit frank feedback from current LTCs about barriers to collaboration and try to address those concerns before establishing sharing platforms.

CHAPTER SEVEN

Language Training Center Costs and Resources

The LTC Program is a grant-based program that funds centers based in IHEs to provide instruction to military personnel. The funding process involves an RFP that details the requirements of the program. Centers respond with proposals that detail their plans for instruction along with their funding requests. Centers request funds for their various needs, including instructional materials and salaries for instructors. Many centers have different methods for paying instructors and have different needs regarding materials and resources. While the data available were not sufficient for a complete and thorough cost analysis, and the variety of offerings within the LTC Program did not allow for a cost effectiveness analysis, we were able to use the descriptive data gathered in this study to draw a number of insights about the costs and resources associated with running the LTC Program more generally. In this chapter, we describe how LTCs receive funding from DLNSEO and IIE, some of the costs associated with providing training, and the extent to which LTCs are using the resources available. We also look at capacity utilization across the LTC Program, because it reflects the extent to which DoD partners are taking advantage of the training opportunities funded through the grants.

The Request-for-Proposals Process

The process to receive a grant to become an LTC requires that experts at IHEs partner with a DoD entity and submit a proposal. The process begins with an RFP that is created through a collaborative effort between DLNSEO and IIE. While DLNSEO sets the overall program guidelines, IIE provides support and advice in the process and ultimately administers the RFP.

The RFP includes several criteria that the LTCs must meet and describe in their proposals: a DoD operational requirement, training tailored to meet the specified operational requirements, capacity to deliver the specified training, training delivery approaches that meet the requirements of DoD personnel, training that will yield measurable language skills across modalities, assessment results of language training, and institutional commitment. The RFP includes a comprehensive overview of the requirements of the program and description of how the proposals will be evaluated. As part of the proposal, centers submit a budget detailing how they will allocate their funds.

Once proposals are submitted, a panel of academic and DoD representatives evaluates them based on the criteria. The reviewers, convened by IIE, discuss and rank the proposals and make recommendations to IIE. DoD approves final funding decisions subject to availability of funding.

The grant sizes vary throughout the program. The RFP for 2016–2017 states the expectation that grant requests fall between $200,000 and $1,500,000. Actual grant sizes for that year ranged from $250,000 to just below $2,000,000. In 2016, proposals were due in March, with notifications of awards in June. The grant year began August 1, 2016, and ended July 31, 2017.

Overhead Rates

All of the nine LTCs must pay a portion of their grant to their host institutions. These rates are set by the universities and not by DoD. Eight of the nine pay a percentage overhead rate, and one pays a fixed dollar amount that is not a percentage. Overhead rates vary based on the percentage of courses held on campus versus off campus. Five of the LTCs have a 26-percent overhead rate because the majority of, if not all, courses are held off campus. One LTC explained that if the center held more than 50 percent of its courses on campus, its rate would increase from 26 percent to 51 percent. One center's overhead rate recently decreased from 59.5 percent to 38.4 percent because it changed from offering three of seven courses off campus to five of seven courses off campus. Of the two LTCs that have the majority of courses on campus, their overhead rates are 47.5 percent and 51 percent. The overhead rates typically apply to all aspects of the grant. However, three LTCs did state that the overhead does not apply to costs designated as student support, which include tuition fees for college credit.

Of the nine LTCs, only three have to pay for classroom space, and one of these has to pay only for space for courses that are offered off campus. The center that does not have an overhead percentage rate pays $600 per training day for facility use. Another LTC leases a space because of lack of classroom and office space at the university.

Common Expenditures

Below are common expenses for LTCs.

Staff and Instructor Salaries

A portion of each LTC's award goes toward the salaries for the management, general staff, and instructors. The management includes the principal investigators and the program directors. These salaries can vary greatly depending on part-time or full-time status. Most LTCs employ additional staff to assist with running the program. These can include program assistants, administrative assistants, pedagogy specialists, finance coordinators, military liaisons, and technology specialists. A portion of the grant also pays for the instructors. Instructor salaries vary greatly across the LTCs. Depending on the LTC, instructors may be paid hourly, weekly, or by course.

Instructional Materials

Instructional materials include textbooks, lesson guides, office supplies, movies, audio resources, and cultural resources such as games and food. The costs of instructional materials vary by LTC. Two LTCs reported that they do not spend funds on instructional materials. One of those two uses only open-source materials for instruction. Six of the nine LTCs reported that they do spend money on instructional materials, and they provided some information on those costs. Four of them reported their instructional materials cost *per student,* and the costs ranged from $48 to $437, depending on the LTC and the actual course. Two of the LTCs reported their instructional materials costs *per course.* These two LTCs' costs per course were $275 and $625. One LTC provided its instructional materials cost *per year,* and the cost was $1,000. One LTC did not provide information on the costs of its instructional materials.

Technology Support

LTCs pay for a variety of technology support. At least two LTCs pay for survey software to create, distribute, and analyze their course evaluation surveys. Two LTCs also pay for computers and computer accessories for their staff. The LTC that delivers VTC courses pays for two-way video systems and managed video services. Three LTCs reported expenditures for online storage systems.

Assessments

Four LTCs reported language assessments as an expenditure. One LTC estimated tests and assessment materials at $75 per student. One LTC stated that a telephonic OPI costs about $140. This LTC reported that while OPI by computer (OPIc) is less costly, OPIcs are not available for all languages, and the LTC believes the scores tend to be lower than on non-computer-based OPIs. Another LTC reported budgeting for OPIcs at the beginning and end of the course.

Travel

Six of the LTCs provided details about travel-related costs. LTCs that provide courses off campus often offer mileage reimbursements to instructors. Travel costs can also include flights, hotel, and per diem costs for trips to the annual meetings, conferences, meetings with DoD partners, or courses that are held a significant distance from the institution.

Classroom Space

Six of the nine LTCs do not pay directly for classroom space. Of the three that do pay for classroom space, one pays only for space for classes offered off campus. Another center conducts an entirely online course and thus does not use classroom space. The center that does not have a fixed overhead percentage rate pays $600 per training day for facility use. Another LTC leases space because of a shortage of classroom and office space available at the university. This center also pays for custodial services for the space.

Unanticipated Factors That Affected Spending

In the 2016–2017 grant year, the majority of LTCs were able to provide training and thus spend funds at or near the level granted; however, some LTCs did not fully spend their budgets. We asked those LTCs about the reasons for underspending. At least three LTCs stated that funds were underspent because of lower enrollment than expected. Two of these LTCs specifically mentioned that lower enrollment resulted in purchasing fewer assessments than were originally estimated in the budget. At least two LTCs underspent because of staff turnover, staff not being hired as expected, or delays in hiring. One LTC underspent because the fringe was lower than expected. One LTC explained that it always budgets for the maximum possible to avoid the possibility of underestimating and later exceeding the budget.

Capacity and Utilization

For each grant year, LTCs plan to offer a certain number of courses with a targeted number of students enrolled in those courses, and they request funding based on these numbers. To determine the extent to which DoD partners were taking advantage of the training capacity available through the LTCs, we examined the numbers of courses offered by each LTC, the targeted class size for the courses, and the numbers of students who actually enrolled. We found that some of the spaces available were not being filled. While it is not reasonable to expect all seats to be filled across the program, the proportion of unutilized spaces at some LTCs presents an opportunity to better utilize the program's capacity and take fuller advantage of courses that are already being provided and paid for. The alternative is that some DoD sponsors may be paying for language training elsewhere, rather than taking advantage of the training available through the LTCs.

In the 2016–2017 grant year, the data provided by the LTCs indicate that more than 200 courses were provided across the LTC Program and that those courses provided approximately 1,950 seats, with about 1,450 of those seats being filled, indicating that about 74 percent of the capacity was utilized program-wide.

Among the nine LTCs, there was a wide range of capacity utilization in courses, from 50 to 100 percent, with a median of 80 percent. Three of the LTCs had capacity utilization of less than 70 percent. It is important to keep in mind that expecting 100-percent capacity utilization across the program is unrealistic, given the uncertainties of service members' schedules and their needs to be responsive to a range of demands. Furthermore, we recognize that the setting of class size targets is flexible and subject to the judgment of each individual LTC. While one LTC might set a target class size of eight for a certain course, another might set a target of six for the same course, and both LTCs could end of up with the same number of students enrolled. Correspondingly, we do not suggest that LTCs should be expected or required to attain 100-percent capacity utilization, and in fact, we would discourage such a requirement. However, these numbers suggest that some LTCs may benefit from assistance in filling the courses they have, and that DoD partners could be made aware of and encouraged to use the available training capacity.

Conclusion

The LTCs use their grant funding to provide instruction to military personnel. The size of each grant reflects the anticipated budget, which is based on providing an estimated amount of training capacity for the grant year. The grant funds pay for overhead, staff, instructors, travel, and instructional resources. While the majority of LTCs are providing the number of training courses at or near the capacity determined by their grant sizes, we found the enrollment in those courses at a small number of LTCs to be below capacity and the level of capacity utilization program-wide to be approximately 74 percent, suggesting that the DoD partners are not taking full advantage of the number of training seats available to them.

With some sites having unfilled seats in existing courses, there is an opportunity to increase the number of students served within the amount of funding provided by the existing grant awards. We found that some LTCs did not spend the entire amount of their awards, due in part to lower than expected enrollment. This suggests that student enrollment could be increased up to the estimated capacity without increasing the cost of the program beyond the amount provided by the existing grant levels. To increase the benefit derived from the existing investments in training, DLNSEO and the LTC Program could look for ways to use existing capacity more fully. For example, the program could consider options for disseminating information about available courses or for sending excess demand from one site to another. Because relationships with DoD partners seem to influence student enrollment, options for additional communication with DoD partners could also be considered.

CHAPTER EIGHT

Operating Within Institutions of Higher Education

Each LTC operates within an IHE. The nature of the relationship with these institutions varies somewhat among the LTCs, with some centers operating more independently and others tied very closely to the university and its academic departments. In this chapter, we describe the advantages and disadvantages reported to us by the LTCs.

Advantages

The LTCs recognized many advantages from their affiliations with IHEs. Several LTCs value having access to the faculty already employed at the affiliated institutions. The institutions have extensive language and other departments from which the LTCs can draw talent. Similarly, IHEs tend to have wide networks of contacts with additional experts outside the institutions.

These institutions also provide centers with infrastructure. One LTC noted that with its fixed price overhead, it has access to reliable facilities and technology. Another center has access to the university's academic resource center, which provides assistance with materials creation and web design support.

Two representatives of IHEs commented that the university affiliation provides their LTCs with added credibility. They believed that community members and guest speakers felt more at ease coming to the university because it is known and trusted. One LTC commented that it is advantageous to be affiliated with a place of higher learning because it provides gravitas in the education field.

Additionally, LTCs noted that the IHE affiliation provides unique opportunities for both the students and the instructors. For instance, a university affiliation makes it possible to offer university credit to students. One LTC stated that if the program is going to offer high-quality education in language and culture, it should use the same standards as courses that qualify for university credit, and being affiliated with a university enables this level of quality. Another LTC believed that the university setting offers military personnel a different and useful perspective. For example, classes might discuss controversial topics, leading to valuable cultural exchanges between military personnel and civilians. Another LTC mentioned that many LTC students had never had the opportunity to study in a university environment before attending LTC courses. Exposing them to university-level instruction may open a door to attending a university, an option that some military members may not have previously considered.

Disadvantages

While the IHE affiliation is beneficial in many ways, the LTCs also reported disadvantages.

Several LTCs mentioned specific challenges with university processes that led to logistical issues. At least two LTCs noted that the university's finance departments were particularly slow. One LTC stated that it was difficult to pay its instructors in a timely manner and that they had seen delays in payment of up to three months. The other LTC has found it challenging to accurately track its spending because the university's financial system was so slow, and this could lead to unspent funds. At least two LTCs noted that the universities have a diffuse bureaucracy, in which actions require many approvals. Another LTC noted that there had been occasional misunderstandings with university administration regarding the LTC financial responsibilities.

One LTC noted particular challenges with the university calendar in relation to the calendar of its partner. This LTC pointed out that the university and the military operate on entirely different calendars. The timeframes when the university can offer the most benefit do not line up with the military's schedule. While the military wants on-demand service, this LTC's instructors are university faculty who have other responsibilities during the school year. This center has the most capacity during the summer, but the DoD partner requests courses intermittently and all year round.

Two LTCs also mentioned challenges with hiring instructors and teaching assistants. One LTC noted that the human resource processes were difficult and protracted. Another LTC told an anecdote about being unable to hire a language tutor due to university requirements that the tutor did not meet, despite being otherwise qualified.

Another challenge lies in the potential disconnect between the university and the mission of the LTC. One LTC felt that its IHE failed to appreciate that the mission of a university can be broader than the general academic mission. This LTC expressed frustration that the university would not allow the LTC's students to use the university kitchen because they were not students of the university. The LTC suggested that since it paid overhead to the university, it should have access to everything that it needs to deliver the courses.

Conclusion

The LTC's affiliations with IHEs provide both advantages and disadvantages. One of the clear advantages is the availability of faculty and experts to use as instructors and speakers. The institutions also provide facilities and technology support; however, not all LTCs are based on the campuses, and not all have dedicated physical locations. Additionally, the university setting allows for a valuable dialogue between military and civilians, providing both military personnel and university faculty with unique opportunities that they may not otherwise experience.

There are also disadvantages. LTCs reported bureaucratic processes, which can lead to delays in both receiving and disbursing payments. Additionally, universities' calendars may not align with those of DoD partners or of DLNSEO.

CHAPTER NINE

Conclusions and Recommendations

In this study, we looked broadly at the activities across the entire LTC Program to provide DLNSEO with insights about its effectiveness, whether the program should be continued, and, if so, opportunities for improvement. Through research that included document review, site visits, and interviews, we examined key aspects of the LTC Program to provide answers to several broad questions. In this chapter, we summarize our findings and conclusions by answering the questions posed in Chapter One, and we recommend ways to strengthen the LTC Program.

Is the LTC Program Fulfilling Its Mandate?

The central objective of the LTC Program, as stated in Section 529 of the FY 2010 NDAA, is to provide language and culture training to DoD personnel. The legislation calls for the program to

- build skills in language and area studies from beginning through advanced levels
- provide language training in critical and strategic languages for operational readiness
- use alternative language training delivery systems
- provide programs that can be incorporated into ROTC
- expand the pool of qualified instructors in critical and strategic languages and regional studies
- facilitate the recruitment of heritage speakers of critical and strategic languages into DoD uniformed and civilian service.

Judging by the data gathered in this study, the LTC Program is fulfilling its mandate. In the 2016–2017 grant year, the program comprised nine centers serving the needs of 24 DoD partners. Through its nine centers, the program provided more than 200 courses to more than 1,450 students in 15 languages as well as regional studies.

We found that the LTC Program is directly addressing the first three of these objectives. Table 2.1 shows the breadth of course offerings across the program. These courses are provided using a variety of delivery systems, including classroom, distance-learning, and immersion. Indirectly, the LTC Program is meeting the fourth and fifth objectives. Although the LTCs are not primarily designed to meet the needs of ROTC, a number of the LTC institutions also serve Project GO, another DLNSEO program geared specifically to serve ROTC, and those sites reported synergies between the two. Regarding building the pool of qualified instructors, the fact that LTCs hire, train, and develop teachers in critical and strategic languages implies that they are strengthening the pool of instructors in these languages. The only objective that the program is not clearly meeting is one that may not be feasible for it to address, and that is to facilitate recruitment of heritage speakers of critical and strategic languages to DoD—however, the fact that speakers of these critical languages are recruited to become teachers for DoD training is perhaps one step in that direction.

How Are LTCs Leveraging Their Institutes of Higher Education?

We found that being situated in IHEs provides LTCs a number of benefits, and LTCs reported taking advantage of these benefits in a number of ways. IHEs provide access to scholars and experts in languages, pedagogy, and area studies, and these experts can become teachers or staff members in the LTCs. Furthermore, several LTCs reported hiring instructors or teaching assistants from the pool of advanced graduate students in their institutions. In doing this, the LTC is not only receiving an advantage by being affiliated with the IHE, it is also contributing to the development of the defense language professional community by giving these instructors more experience teaching in a way that meets the needs of DoD personnel. Most LTCs also leverage their institutions in a fairly obvious way—by utilizing campus facilities for courses and office space. However, whether the courses are offered on campus, at a DoD site such as a military base, or at another location, the LTCs reported that they have immediate credibility with DoD partners and the students they send because of their university affiliation. Among those who attended training at the LTC's IHE, a number of students reported viewing the LTC training more positively because they got to attend on the IHE's campus and felt that doing so was a privilege. Thus, the IHE relationships provide LTCs with networks of expertise, facilities, credibility, and prestige, and the LTCs appear to be leveraging those benefits. However, they do come with trade-offs, such as potentially high overhead costs and bureaucratic processes that, for some LTCs, delay payments, impede the tracking of funding, and inhibit hiring.

What Practices Are in Place, and Where Can They Be Improved?

For this study, we selected a few of the many practices that are important to the effectiveness of LTCs in fulfilling the program's mandate. Given that the program is meant to allow for flexibility and innovation, we were not surprised to find a wide variety in courses, styles of training, and approaches to key aspects of implementation, such as ensuring teaching quality, measuring performance, and use of grant funds.

We will focus here on teaching and address measurement and use of funds in the answers to the two questions that follow.

LTC teaching quality is crucially important because it directly affects the outcomes of the students who attend LTC training. LTCs reported a variety of approaches to screening, developing, and evaluating their teachers. Although teaching quality appears to be strong at the LTCs, as reported by LTC directors, DoD partners, and students, we observed some opportunities for improvement related to their supervision, evaluation, and professional development and collaboration across the LTC Program. We found that LTCs vary widely in how they train and evaluate their instructors, which suggests that a variety of standards and expectations are being applied when thinking about the quality of teaching. We also heard that some teachers felt the need to develop their own materials, and some were not aware that other LTCs were offering similar courses. Furthermore, some others expressed a reluctance to share information with other teachers or other LTCs. These findings suggest opportunities to improve the way teaching is evaluated and the way teachers are professionally developed, while also fostering a collaborative professional community program-wide. We provide some options for doing so below in the recommendations.

How Can the Program Improve Its Metrics and Assessments?

While DLNSEO, IIE, and the LTCs all recognize the importance of measuring outcomes, they do it in different ways. Variation is to be expected (and even desired) due to the nature of the LTC Program, but there are some areas in which consistency could be encouraged, where appropriate. In addition to the variation we observed in how LTCs evaluate their teachers' performance, we found substantial variation in the ways that LTCs measure other performance—of their students and of their centers overall. We do not recommend requiring specific student outcome metrics program-wide, because we believe they would run counter to the program's intended flexibility, but there is an opportunity to provide guidance and recommendations to help LTCs identify appropriate, measurable, and meaningful outcomes that suit their individual centers. There is also an opportunity to leverage the surveys that all LTCs are already conducting to begin collecting program-wide data from students and possibly DoD partners for the first time. We discuss measurement further in the recommendations below.

What Factors Affect How the LTCs Use Their Funds?

LTCs use their funding for a variety of expenses. In the 2016–17 grant year, the majority of LTCs were able to provide training and thus spend funds at or near the level granted; however, some LTCs did not fully spend their budgets. Although some underspending was associated with challenges in hiring or with university bureaucracy, the most common explanation was lower-than-expected student enrollment. While the majority of LTCs are providing the number of courses at or near the capacity determined by their grant sizes, we found the enrollment in those courses at a small number of LTCs to be below capacity, suggesting that the DoD partners are not taking full advantage of the training available to them, despite positive perceptions of the quality of the training.

Recommendations

Foster a Greater Ongoing Program-Wide Focus on Meaningful Outcomes, Not Just Provision of Training

With the LTC Program now well established in its eighth year of operation, there is an opportunity to strengthen the program and ensure its positive impact by increasing the focus on the outcomes of its training rather than merely on the provision of training. The program has demonstrated its ability to provide hundreds of courses per year to meet the needs of 24 DoD partners and more than 1,450 students in a single grant year.[1] A next step in the program's development could be for it to place further emphasis on the importance of measuring training outcomes and to use the information to engage in deliberate and ongoing cycles of continuous improvement.

At the time of the study, in 2017, some LTCs were assessing their own performance through assessments of student outcomes, and others were doing so primarily by whether or not they had provided the training requested of them. Furthermore, the LTC Program overall reports its outcomes in terms of provision—that is, numbers of courses provided and numbers of students served. While this is a reasonable first step, we recommend that DLNSEO and IIE now consider reporting its success in terms of the student outcomes obtained. For example, the program provided *x* training courses, serving *y* students, with *z* percent of students reaching the targeted learning or proficiency goals, as measured by the methods collaboratively identified by the LTC and IIE. This would allow the LTCs and DLNSEO to report not only the extent to which they provided training but also the extent to which the training accomplished its goals.

As mentioned earlier, the variety of goals among the LTCs makes it unlikely that there will be a single set of measurable outcomes that apply neatly to all. The LTCs

---

[1] IIE, 2017.

vary in the languages they teach (and they do not all teach languages), the levels of proficiency they target, the purposes of their training, and DoD partners they serve. A more feasible approach may be to encourage each LTC to articulate objectives that go beyond provision and represent meaningful training outcomes for the DoD partners and students. This process could be done initially through a pilot phase dedicated to identifying appropriate, meaningful, and measurable outcomes for the respective centers. Following the pilot phase, identifying and reporting measures of success could become a requirement stated in the RFP and implemented through the course of normal program activities. Although the most recent RFP requested plans for measurement, the plans have not always been implemented. Moving forward, identifying and measuring meaningful outcomes could serve as foundation for continuous improvement.

Because it is unlikely that any single outcome measure will apply to all nine LTCs, DLNSEO and IIE should also consider developing a small number of survey questions to be included in the course evaluation surveys administered by each LTC. This would leave the LTCs free to design their course evaluation surveys, as they have always been, while also providing DLNSEO with valuable program-wide data that would allow for analysis across the LTC Program.

Over Time, Encourage and Build a Culture of Professional Collaboration Among LTCs

We observed that LTCs currently have little interaction with one another outside of the program's annual meeting. Many LTCs expressed interest in the practices of others but perceived little to no means of learning more about them. Importantly, we noticed an undercurrent of competition that was confirmed by members of the LTC community. At the same time, we observed that some LTCs have more demand for their training than they can accommodate, while other LTCs are under-enrolled. In addition, we saw teachers at various sites working independently on efforts such as developing course materials, sometimes unaware that others were doing nearly the same thing in other LTCs, and sometimes aware but suspicious of collaborating for fear of losing control of their intellectual property.

Although it is not possible nor recommended to require collaboration, we recommend that DLNSEO and IIE take steps to foster and build it over time. Options include providing more in-person meetings, not only for LTC directors but also for their instructional leaders and teaching staffs. Productive purposes for such meetings could be to provide professional development for instructors teaching similar courses at various sites; training for specific certifications, such as OPI tester training; or workshops in materials development for teachers of languages in which materials are especially limited. Another option would be to incentivize and recognize staff members from more-established and demonstrably successful LTCs who provide coaching, mentoring, and/or guidance to staff members at newer LTCs. Such steps that enhance collaboration and professional learning program-wide may begin to reduce the underlying sense of competition over time, leading to a professional community more likely to sustain itself if and when the grant program is reduced or ended.

Explore Ways to Help DoD Partners More Fully Utilize the Training Capacity Provided

The LTC Program represents a substantial investment in providing language and culture training to DoD in a way that is flexible and allows for innovation to meet new and changing needs. Program-wide, we found that about 74 percent of the training seats available are being filled. At individual LTCs, the percentage of available seats that are filled ranges from 50 to 100 percent, with a median of 80 percent, revealing that in some LTCs, a substantial amount of the capacity for language and culture training is not being utilized. Most commonly, LTCs attributed the lower enrollment numbers simply to DoD partners sending fewer students than the DoD partners originally projected. This could be due to students canceling at the last minute because of job demands, to courses being offered at inconvenient times, or to a DoD partner overestimating the demand for a course they requested. It could also be due to a center responding to a request for a course in a critical language for which the demand is small, perhaps only two or three students in a course that could have accommodated five or six. When class sizes are intentionally small, as they are in LTCs, having just one or two students not enroll as planned can make a substantial difference when it happens repeatedly. We note that it is unrealistic to expect 100-percent capacity utilization and do not recommend setting requirements in this regard.

To date, LTCs have held the sole responsibility to ensure that their courses are filled, and the LTCs with lower enrollment reported their concerted efforts in this regard. We recommend that the LTC Program look to establish a means to share information about available training with a broader range of DoD entities so that if the DoD partner that requested the training does not fill the available spaces, other DoD personnel would be able to enroll. Over time, this could lead to greater awareness of LTC training and perhaps to new partnerships and/or increased interest in LTC training. Further, the program should consider offering more support to under-enrolled LTCs, both to establish stronger DoD partnerships and to more easily communicate the training opportunity to other DoD entities in addition to their specific partner.

Looking Ahead

The LTC Program was created to provide language and culture training to DoD personnel from beginning to advanced levels in order to sustain and enhance operational readiness in critical languages, culture, and regional expertise. In the eight years since its inception, the program has grown from five centers to nine and demonstrated its ability to provide quality training in a responsive and flexible manner to an increasingly larger population of DoD students, serving more than 1,450 in the 2016–2017 grant year.[2] The challenges that lie ahead will be to (1) encourage increased consistency across the program in areas where it makes sense while still providing opportunities for uniqueness and creativity at each of the LTCs and (2) increase meaningful measurement of outcomes while continuing to support responsiveness, innovation, and, potentially, further growth. The findings of this study should provide LTC policymakers, leaders, staff members, and partners with a base of information to help them successfully plan for and execute the next stage in the development of this critical DoD program.

---

2 IIE, 2017.

APPENDIX A

Student Interview and Focus Group Questions

Interview and Focus Group Questions for LTC Students

Before Training

1. What led you to take a course at this center?
2. What had to happen in order for you to be able to attend here?
3. Did you have to request permission to attend? Who had to approve it?
4. Did someone else have to nominate you to attend?

During Training

1. What has your experience been like since you have been here?
2. To what extent is this course meeting your needs?
3. What are some of the things you like about the course?
4. What do you recommend improving?

After Training

1. What do you expect to do with what you learn here?
2. How will this affect your job?
3. How useful do you expect it to be?
4. How often will you use it?

Other

1. Anything else we have not talked about that you think is important?

APPENDIX B

Instructor Interview and Focus Group Questions

Interview and Focus Group Questions for LTC Instructors

Background

1. Please tell us a little bit about your background, education, and teaching experience.
2. How long have you been with the program?
3. Are you employed full time or part time?

LTC Mission, Objectives, and Metrics

1. How would you describe your LTC's mission and objectives? How do you contribute to these objectives?
2. How do you know if you're meeting the LTC overall objectives?

Program and Course Design

1. What metrics do you collect? Can you share any of them with us?
2. How are the courses that you teach designed? Do you design the course? Do you use DLI or some other curriculum?
3. How much information does your partner provide you about your students' operational futures (what the unit's operational needs for language are)?
4. Do you tailor the courses to meet your partner's operational needs?

Capacity and Throughput

1. What is the current instructor-to-student ratio in your classes?
2. How many classes do you teach each year?
3. What is your typical class size (number of students)?
4. How many students do you teach each year?

5. How many students could you teach each year, given the language and program you teach?

Teacher and Student Performance Outcomes

1. How were you recruited? (from the broader labor market or from this institution)
2. How is your performance measured and evaluated?
3. How does the LTC assist in your curriculum development, teaching, professional development, and professional career?
4. How do you measure student performance?
5. Do you pre-test your students? Do you adjust courses according to need?
6. How do you evaluate student outcomes from the courses you teach? How do you determine the level a student has attained from taking your course?
7. What data do you collect on students? Can you share aggregated (not identifiable) data with us?

Operations

1. How does being part of a college or university facilitate your teaching in an LTC?
2. Are there any ways in which being part of a college or university makes your job more difficult?

Recommendations for Improvement

1. Are there any limiting factors that you feel hinder your ability to produce desired outcomes?
2. Are there any ways in which you would like to improve your work at the LTC? What would enable you to make those changes?
3. Do you have any recommendations for strengthening or improving the LTC Program at your school?

Other Stakeholders

1. Are there any other stakeholders you recommend we communicate with?

APPENDIX C

DoD Partner Interview Questions

Interview Questions for DoD Partners

1. How did you become partnered with [name of institution] for language training through the DLNSEO LTC Program?
2. Did you approach them, or did they approach you?
3. How long did it take to solidify the relationship through any necessary formal channels, and how easy or difficult was that process?
4. How do you communicate your specific needs to the LTC?
5. How often do you communicate with the staff at the LTC?
6. How do you identify the individuals to be sent for training at the LTC? What factors play into the decisions for whom to send?
7. How important is the training to your organization? [Or other term, such as "squadron," "unit," "brigade," etc., as appropriate.]
8. How do you think these individuals view the training? [To clarify, you may need to provide examples, such as: As an honor, an important part of building/maintaining skills, a burden, interference with their regular jobs, etc.]
9. How does the LTC let you know what training courses it is offering and the number of spaces available? And how easy or difficult is it for you to fill those spaces?
10. To what extent is the LTC meeting your language training needs?
11. What are the most valuable aspects of the LTC Program?
12. What, if anything, would you recommend changing to improve the LTC Program?
13. Have you ever partnered with another LTC?

APPENDIX D

Language Training Center Administrator Interview Questions

Interview Questions for Language Training Center Directors and Staff

Background Information

First, we'd like to go over some background information about your LTC. (We have much of this information from other sources, so this is essentially to confirm what we have and fill in any blanks.)

- When this LTC was first established
- Languages taught
- Course titles
- Levels taught (aiming to get students from ILR _____ to _____)
- Covering which skills (L/R/S/W)
- Delivery methods
- Partner(s)
- Students (from which organization, at what career stage or level)
- Purpose or goal of the training (Why do these students need the training?)
- Do the courses teach any native or heritage speakers of the language(s)?

LTC Mission, Objectives, and Metrics

1. How would you describe your LTC's mission and objectives?
2. How do you know if you're meeting these objectives?
3. How do you define and measure success?
4. What metrics do you collect? Can you share any of them with us?

Program and Course Design

1. How do you design the courses that your LTC provides?
2. How much information does your partner provide you about their operational needs?

3. How do you tailor the courses to meet your partner's operational needs?
4. Do you use any existing instructional materials, or do you develop them at the center?

Capacity and Throughput

1. What is the current instructor-to-student ratio?
2. How many courses do you provide each year?
3. What is the typical class size (number of students)?
4. How many students do you serve each year?
5. How many students could you serve each year, given the current funding provided?

Teacher and Student Performance and Outcomes

1. How do you recruit and hire your teachers? (from the broader labor market or from your institution)
2. How do you measure and evaluate their performance?
3. How do you measure student performance?
4. How do you evaluate student outcomes from LTC courses?
5. What data do you collect on students? Can you share aggregated (not identifiable) data with us?

Operations

1. How does being part of a college or university facilitate running an LTC?
2. Are there any ways in which being part of a college or university makes your job more difficult?

Funding and Costs

1. What is the amount of your LTC grant, and what are the start and end dates of the grant period?
2. What is your annual budget?
3. What is the average cost to provide a course?
4. What would you estimate is the cost per student?

[We will follow up with you again to discuss costs further.]

Recommendations for Improvement

5. Are there any limiting factors that you feel hinder your ability to produce desired outcomes?
6. Are there any ways in which you would like to improve or grow your LTC? What would enable you to make those changes?
7. Do you have any recommendations for strengthening or improving the LTC Program overall?
8. Do you have any specific recommendations for IIE or DLNSEO with regard to the LTC Program?

Other Stakeholders

1. Please provide the contact information for your partners.
2. Are there any other stakeholders you recommend we communicate with?

APPENDIX E

DLNSEO Leadership and Staff Interview Questions

Interview Questions for DLNSEO Director and Staff

Interaction with the LTCs

1. In your role, how much interaction do you have with the LTCs? And for what purpose or on what topics?
2. How would you characterize the relationship between the LTCs and DLNSEO?
3. How often do you communicate with the LTCs and how do you communicate with them?
4. How often do the LTCs communicate with you?
5. How satisfied are you with the extent and quality of the communication between you and the LTCs?

Program Administration and the DLNSEO Grant Process

1. How would you describe the role of IIE?
2. How much of the processes for grant proposals and awards are determined by DLNSEO and how much by IIE?
3. Are the selection criteria determined by DLNSEO or IIE? If they're written, from whom can we get a copy? If not written, can you tell us what they are?
4. Are there externally mandated limiting factors (budget size, number of institutions, etc.)? If so, what are they?
5. Who determines the grant sizes and how? (Who does this, DLNSEO or IIE?)
6. What parts of the relationship with IIE are going especially well, and are there any aspects you would like to see improved?

Performance

1. Has DLNSEO set specific goals or objectives for the LTCs?
2. How does DLNSEO know if the LTCs are meeting these objectives/goals?
3. How does DLNSEO define and measure success across the LTC Program?

4. Are there any limiting factors that you feel hinder DLNSEO's ability to produce the desired outcomes from the LTC Program?
5. We have seen the LTC activity tracker, and we understand that IIE collects these data. Which metrics do you think are the most important?
6. Which metrics, if any, are shared with the LTCs?

Strategic Vision for LTCs

1. What is your strategic vision for the future of LTCs?
2. What do you consider the key strengths of the LTC Program?
3. What do you perceive as weaknesses of the program, if any?
4. What opportunities exist for the LTC Program that have not yet been tapped into?
5. Do you perceive any threats to the success of the LTC Program?
6. Are there any ways in which you would like to improve or change the LTC Program in the short or long term?

APPENDIX F

IIE Leadership and Staff Interview Questions

Interview Questions for IIE Staff

Interaction with the LTCs

1. What is your position at IIE?
2. In your position, what are your roles and responsibilities with respect to the LTC Program overall? To individual LTCs?
3. How much personal interaction do you have with DLNSEO regarding the LTC Program? And for what purpose or on what topics?
4. How much interaction do you have with the LTCs? And for what purpose or on what topics?
5. How would you characterize the relationship between the IIE and the LTCs?
6. How would you characterize the relationship between the IIE and DLNSEO?
7. How often do you communicate with the LTCs and how do you communicate with them?
8. How often do the LTCs communicate with you?
9. How satisfied are you with the extent and quality of the communication between you and the LTCs?

Program Administration and the DLNSEO Grant Process

1. The IIE website says, "The Institute of International Education administers the Language Training Centers program on behalf of the Defense Language and National Security Education Office." How would you describe the organizational role of IIE with regard to administration of the LTC Program? What does "administration" encompass?
2. To what extent is IIE responsible for developing or managing processes for grant proposals and awards? To what extent is DLNSEO responsible?
3. Are the selection criteria determined by DLNSEO or IIE? We understand they are articulated in the RFP. Are there any selection criteria that are not in the RFP?

4. Are there externally mandated limiting factors (budget size, number of institutions, etc.)? If so, what are they?
5. Who determines the individual grant sizes and how? (Who does this, DLNSEO or IIE?)
6. What parts of the relationship with DLNSEO are going especially well? Are there any aspects you would like to see improved?
7. What parts of the relationship with the LTCs are going especially well? Are there any aspects you would like to see improved?

Performance

1. Has DLNSEO or IIE set specific goals or objectives for the LTC Program? For individual LTCs?
2. How does IIE know if the LTCs are meeting these objectives/goals?
3. How does IIE define and measure success across the LTC Program?
4. Are there any limiting factors that you feel hinder IIE's ability to support the LTCs in their effort to produce the desired outcomes from the LTC Program?
5. We have seen the LTC activity tracker, and we understand that IIE collects these data. How do you use the data?
6. Which metrics do you think are the most important?
7. Which metrics, if any, do you share with the LTCs? With DLNSEO?

Strategic Vision for LTCs

1. What do you think is the main purpose of the LTC Program?
2. What do you consider the key strengths of the LTC Program?
3. What do you perceive as weaknesses of the program, if any?
4. What opportunities exist for the LTC Program that have not yet been tapped into?
5. Given budget and resource increases, could the LTC Program be scaled to include more institutions? What is the upper limit for potential growth considering current and future sponsor needs?
6. Do you perceive any threats to the success of the LTC Program?
7. Are there any ways in which you would recommend changing or improving the LTC Program?

APPENDIX G

Program Costs: Language Training Center Administrative Interview Questions

DLNSEO LTC Program Cost Interview Questions

LTC Directors and Administrators

Please answer the questions below to the best of your ability. You may add the information directly into this Word document, create a table, or use an Excel spreadsheet—whatever is easiest for you. Thank you.

Instructional Time and Teacher's Time

1. Please provide a list of each course you conducted in the last complete grant year, and a list of each course you plan to offer in the current grant year. For each year, indicate the number of times you provided each course. If the conduct of a course differed substantially between one offering and another (for example, Advanced Russian was 80 hours when offered in October and 120 hours when offered in January), then list those instances as two separate courses, noting the difference between the two.
2. How many hours of instructional time comprise each course? Over how many days? Does the course include learning activities outside of the classroom, such as field trips, cultural activities, etc.? If yes, please include these hours in the number of hours of instructional time.

Costs of Instruction

1. How many hours of in-class instructor time are required for each course? (If the answers differ among courses, please provide the requested information for each of the various types of courses.)
2. How many hours of preparation time are instructors expected to spend outside of class?
3. How many instructors are assigned to each course?

4. How many teaching assistants (if any) are assigned to each course? (If assignment of teaching assistants varies, please describe the criteria for assigning teaching assistants.)
5. What is your LTC's target for teacher-to-student ratio?
6. Are instructors paid by salary or hourly? How much are instructors paid?
7. How much are teaching assistants paid? Salary or hourly?
8. Are there any other individuals hired to support courses? What are their job titles and responsibilities? How much are they paid?
9. What are the costs for instructional materials?
10. Are there any other costs incurred directly for providing LTC courses?

Facility Costs and Other Indirect Costs

1. Does the college or university charge the LTC overhead? If so, what is the overhead rate? To what do the overhead charges apply? (In other words, is overhead charged for the entire LTC grant or only to certain portions?)
2. Does your LTC have to pay for classroom space? What is the cost of classroom space?
3. Does the LTC pay for any additional support? Such as for information technology or other resources? What are the items and the associated costs?

Course Costs

1. Do you have an estimate of the overall cost to offer a course? If so, what is it? What are the inputs used to calculate it?
2. Are there any other costs that have not been mentioned? If yes, please describe and tell us how much your LTC has spent on those items for each grant year for which you have the data.

Grant Funding

1. Please tell us the amount of grant funds that have been awarded to your LTC for each of the grant years your center has been part of the LTC Program. If there was an initial award followed by a subsequent award in the same grant year, report the two amounts, along with the total for that year.
2. Of the amount awarded for each year, note how much the LTC spent. If funds were left unspent, please describe the factors that influenced the level of spending.

References

IIE—*See* Institute of International Education.

Institute of International Education, *Language Training Center Overview*, New York, 2017.

Interagency Language Roundtable, "Descriptions of Proficiency Levels," undated. As of April 19, 2018:
http://www.govtilr.org/Skills/ILRscale1.htm

Language Training Center Program, "About LTC," webpage, undated (a). As of April 19, 2018:
http://www.dodltc.org/about-ltc

———, "History," webpage, undated (b). As of April 20, 2018:
http://www.dodltc.org/history

———, "Request for Proposal: Language Training Center Program Sponsored by the Defense Language and National Security Education Office—Application Guidelines," 2016.

LTC Program—*See* Language Training Center Program.

Mason, Leah, and Haworth, Bethany, *Leveraging Language and Cultural Education and U.S. Higher Education Programs*, New York: Institute of International Education, April 2011.

National Security Education Program, *2011 Annual Report*, Washington, D.C.: U.S. Department of Defense, 2011.

———, *2012 Annual Report*, Washington, D.C.: U.S. Department of Defense, 2012.

———, *2015 Annual Report*, Washington, D.C.: U.S. Department of Defense, 2015.

Public Law 111-84, National Defense Authorization Act for Fiscal Year 2010, October 28, 2009.

Under Secretary of the Defense for Personnel and Readiness, *Defense Language Transformation Roadmap*, Washington, D.C.: U.S. Department of Defense, 2005. As of April 20, 2018:
http://www.dtic.mil/docs/citations/ADB313370

U.S. Department of Defense, *Language Training Center Program: Report to Congress* (as required by Section 529(e) of the National Defense Authorization Act for Fiscal Year 2010), Washington, D.C., 2013.

Index

CPSIA information can be obtained
at www.ICGtesting.com
Printed in the USA
BVHW011212170619
551200BV00008B/938/P

9 781977 402424